Splash
the
Living Water

**Books by Esther Burroughs
available from New Hope Publishers**

◆

Engraved by Grace

Treasures of a Grandmother's Heart

Empowered

A Garden Path to Mentoring

Splash the Living Water

*Sharing Jesus
in Everyday Moments*

ESTHER BURROUGHS

new
hope
PUBLISHERS

Birmingham, Alabama

New Hope® Publishers
P. O. Box 12065
Birmingham, AL 35202-2065
www.newhopepublishers.com

Library of Congress Cataloging-in-Publication Data

Burroughs, Esther.
  Splash the living water : sharing Jesus in everyday moments / by
Esther Burroughs.
  p. cm.
  Originally published: Nashville : T. Nelson, c1999.
  ISBN 1-59669-002-X (softcover)
  1. Christian women—Religious life. 2. Female friendship—Religious
aspects—Christianity. I. Title.
  BV4527.B8694 2006
  248.8'43—dc22
      2005029227

ISBN: 1-59669-002-X

N064129 • 0406 • 6M1

dedication

To my man for these past 47 years,

Bob Lloyd Burroughs,

father to our daughter, Melody Burroughs Reid,

and our son, David Lloyd Burroughs,

and the most awesome grandfather

to our five grandchildren.

Thank you for the hours spent

finessing this manuscript

and, even more,

for your encouragement in my life

and ministry through the years.

*May God our Father
himself and our Master Jesus
clear the road to you!
And may the Master
pour on the love
so it fills your lives
**and splashes over on
everyone around you,**
just as it does from us to you.
May you be infused
with strength and purity,
filled with confidence
in the presence of God our Father
when our Master Jesus
arrives with all his followers.*

—1 Thessalonians 3:11–13
(*The Message*)

contents

acknowledgements

Skip and Kay Reid are the parents
of our son-in-law, Will Reid.
The Reids have a lovely home on
Lake Lure in the North Carolina mountains,
which they graciously allowed us to use
while I was rewriting this book.
It is a beautiful and restful place to work.
We were blessed by their generosity,
and we are most thankful to them
for sharing it with us.

introduction

In 1986, while working in the mission department of the Home Mission Board (now the North American Mission Board), I was invited to consider a position working with women in the evangelism section. I remember this occasion very clearly. After weeks of playing phone tag with Dr. Robert Hamblin, then vice president of the evangelism department, he walked into my office, sat down, and said, "I want to share with you what I believe God is saying to me." A consultant position working with women in the evangelism section had been open for a year, and he offered me that position.

I remember saying, "Sir, if you think I am someone who would get on an airplane and share Jesus, you have the wrong lady."

He asked, "Well how do you share your faith?"

"I am reserved, and I feel most comfortable sharing in friendship/relationship situations, as well as letting people see Christ in me."

"That's just the way I share my faith," he replied.

"Really!" I said, surprised.

As he explained the job responsibility, he listed five requirements of the position. As he listed them, my heart was thinking *maybe*, but my mind was saying *no way*. When I said, "I don't think I'm the right person," he responded, "Well, I do. Will you just pray about it?"

I said, "My only daughter is getting married in four weeks, and I can't do one other thing."

"Not a problem," he said. "I have four weeks of revival and conference meetings; I will pray, and we can talk in four weeks."

I said, "After the wedding, Bob and I are going off for a week ourselves, but after that, I will pray." I really did not want to deal with it.

He left saying, "I know God has led me to you, Esther, so I will pray He will lead your heart to consider this position."

He left my office and I began to cry.

My secretary, Pat Newton, looked in on me and said, "That is awesome, I couldn't help hear. The position fits you perfectly, and you have been seeking God for a new direction,"

"Don't even say that to me," I cried.

As I shared with my family, every one of them said, "That position fits all your gifts and is made for you."

"Don't even say that to me," was my response every time.

Five weeks later, with fear and trembling, I said, "Yes."

What a great opportunity and challenge it was! Imagine, at 50 years of age, being given a brand-new direction in ministry. I have always thought missions and evangelism have the same goal in different packaging. How can I live missionally and not share Christ? How can you share Christ and not meet needs? Jesus did both.

My first assignment was to develop a tool for teaching women how to share their faith from a woman's heart and giftedness. I began by asking God to show me in Scripture an example of Jesus meeting needs and telling the story.

As I read the Gospel of John, I was led to chapter 4 as the right example, though there are many. The Spirit showed me verse 4. Jesus left Judea and departed into Galilee. *"And He had to pass through Samaria"* (John 4:4).

I call that ***going out of your way while you are on your way.***

Think about this. Jesus is with you everyplace you go...His presence is in you in everything you do. How can you **not** take Him with you? You are going to the hairstylist; while you are there, go out of your way to speak a word on God's behalf. It may be a word of encouragement or thanks expressed for something in your life. It will bless and encourage others.

This book is not about a memorized presentation; it is about a love relationship with Jesus flowing out of your unique essence and giftedness through the Holy Spirit's power. *The Message* states this principle clearly in 1 Thessalonians 3:11–13 (bold italics by author):

> *May God our Father himself and our Master*
> *Jesus clear the road to you! And may the*
> *Master pour on the love so it fills your lives*
> ***and splashes over on everyone around***
> ***you,*** *just as it does from us to you. May you*
> *be infused with strength and purity, filled with*

confidence in the presence of God our Father
when our Master Jesus arrives with all his
followers.

     —1 Thessalonians 3:11–13 *(The Message)*

Jump in, the water's fine! Splash God's love on those in your circle of influence.

and she was thirsty

The early afternoon heat covered her like a damp blanket. Yet the task ahead kept the woman's feet plodding wearily toward the well at the edge of the village. She was aware that everyone in the village of Sychar knew her story. It was, perhaps, their story.

The well was the town gathering place. Jacob, a local hero from centuries ago, had bought this property and had given it to his son. This well had watered Jacob's family, his cattle, and his workmen. The well now belonged to the community.

I wonder, did she ever think about the One who provided this water and the care He had for His people?

She had made the journey to the well many times. Some days she may have wished the time would come when she would never have to return to the well. She did not like to visit the well. She dreaded the trip every time she had to go.

The time at the well was a community time, when village women shared family news and events. They talked about "women things": food, husbands, children, and gossip! (You remember—like those times when you had to do your laundry at the local laundromat!) But the village women's community had no place for this Samaritan woman. She was currently sleeping with someone she was not married to—perhaps the husband or boyfriend of one of the women who came to the well. She knew they did not approve of her and probably talked about her. Most women went in the cool of the morning, but to avoid their gossip and stares, this woman went at noon, when it was very hot.

Did the women in her city have any idea of the nagging emptiness in her life or her personal thirst? Did any of them ever wonder about her loneliness? If anyone asked about her needs that day at the well, she might not have been able to tell them. She might not have known herself. What was she searching for as she moved from relationship to relationship—and from man to man? Did she want children? Was she longing for a close friend? Maybe she desired a family and the opportunity to belong to a real community. Or...maybe she was just resigned to another day of drudgery without hope. Here is her story (to read this in the Bible, see John 4:6–15).

Jesus, weary from His long journey, was sitting by this well to rest. He was tired and thirsty. At His request, the disciples had gone into the village to buy food for their meal.

Jesus must have cherished this moment alone. Approaching footsteps interrupted his thoughts. Seeing the Samaritan woman, Jesus said these simple words to her as she began to draw water from the well: *"Give Me a drink."*

The woman replied, *"How is it that You, being a Jew, ask me for a drink since I am a Samaritan woman?"* She knew the rules. She understood the culture. In those days, men did not speak to women in public, especially at the town watering hole! In addition, Jews had nothing to do with Samaritans—period.

The answer Jesus gave was gentle and inviting. He explained that He was the *"gift of God,"* and that if she asked, He could give her *"living water."*

She must have looked Him over very carefully, questioning His statement, and at the same time, aware that He did not have a dipper with which to draw the water. Was she thinking about the depth of the well—perhaps as deep as her troubled life? Even in her concern about His lack of well-drawing equipment, she seemed to be drawn to Him—yet she was confused by the truth of His words. Choosing to rush on, she asked Him this

19

question: *"Where...do You get that living water? You are not greater than our father Jacob, are You?"*

How quickly Jesus drew her into conversation about earthly and spiritual matters! He knew the thirst of her heart. He probably paused—giving her time to prepare for His answer. Perhaps by now He had begun to address her by name. He said: *"Everyone who drinks of this water will thirst again; but whoever drinks of the water that I will give him shall never thirst; but the water that I will give him will become in him a well of water springing up to eternal life."*

About that time, she must have put down her water pot by the well. How significant were her actions. Perhaps she was beginning to trust this stranger. She said: *"Sir, give me this water, so I will not be thirsty nor come all the way here to draw."*

Could she have realized she was putting the empty pot down in exchange for the living, never-ending, thirst-quenching, eternal life water—hoping against hope that she would never have to come to this dreaded well again? She was right in asking for the living water. He was correct—she indeed would never know spiritual thirst again. Little did she realize that she would never visit Jacob's well again without remembering this life-changing conversation.

And She Was Thirsty

The phone rang. I answered. It was one of my husband's choir members calling to ask a favor. At that time Bob was minister of music at a church. The caller said that a lady from his office had just moved into the townhouse community where we lived. He said she really needed a friend and gave me her townhouse number.

Because of my travel schedule, it was quite some time before I was able to knock on her door. However, the opportunity finally came for me to drop by her home, and I introduced myself by saying that I was a friend of her office worker friend. We stood at the doorstep and talked. After all, why should she trust me? I'm sure we both wondered if we had anything at all in common.

Feeling a bit awkward, I told her I traveled a great deal, but when I was at home, I tried to walk every day. At that time, we lived right next to the street where the movie *Driving Miss Daisy* was being filmed. It was a beautiful place to walk—shady, tall trees, and cool breezes. I invited her into my world by asking if she would walk with me one day soon. She agreed and we followed through. After every walk, we were both thirsty and ready for a drink. As we began a journey together, I should have suspected that God would draw her to His life-giving water in me.

During the next year, we walked as often as our schedules allowed. A friendship soon developed. I learned about her family of origin, and she learned about mine. This precious woman was literally dying of thirst—thirst for the real life. She had a thirst for meaning…a thirst from emptiness. She knew about abuse; she knew about the power of alcohol; she knew about failure; she knew about divorce. She was struggling to make some sense of life. I could feel her thirst, and I wanted to show her the way to the well. She let me know immediately that she wasn't looking for a church! She had tried the church when she was young but did not find what she was looking for there. So...I became her church. She kept saying, "You seem to be so peaceful."

We opened our home to her. She was included in our evenings at the symphony. My husband is a wonderful gourmet cook, and since she also loved to cook, this became an event for us—and I was the beneficiary! Her journey to the well was up and down—three steps forward and two steps back. Like the woman at the well, she made many trips to the well just to get enough water to survive for the day.

Finally the day came! She knocked on my door. She showed up with a Bible in her hands, put her empty life down in front of me, and said, "I want to know the peace you have."

And She Was Thirsty

On several occasions, Bob and I had watched a little red sports car and a BMW pull in and out of the driveway of another beautiful home in our community. To be honest, we wondered how a newlywed couple could live in such a nice place.

Often, as I opened the front door to get the morning paper, I would notice a very well-dressed woman—briefcase in hand—step into her car and drive off.

I wondered what kind of work she did. A quiet voice whispered: *She needs you.*

I argued with that voice, explaining my uncompleted list for that day and a busy schedule for the week; I even pretended I would do it the next week when I returned from my next extended trip.

Two months later, I had the same experience, and once again, I rationalized with that inner voice. I was on my way to speak to a Christian women's conference—to teach them how to splash the living water. (How many times have I missed an everyday opportunity, a divine appointment, to splash the living water in obedience to the Spirit of God?)

Several weeks later, I opened our front door to get the Saturday paper. My neighbor was standing there—ready to ring the doorbell. We were both surprised, and she said, "I'm looking for a man." I said, "My man's not here! And besides I don't share, you understand." We both laughed! I knew a divine interruption was being placed in my Saturday schedule. "May I help?" I asked her.

She said, "I'm trying to get a stationary bike from my car trunk to the upstairs bedroom."

"Oh, I can help you do that," I offered. I'd been dying to see the inside of her lovely home anyway, and this was my chance! So off we went.

Not knowing this neighbor very well, I inquired what she did, explaining that I'd seen her leave each morning with briefcase in hand. She told me that she worked in a professional office in downtown Atlanta.

Then it was her turn. She had seen the taxi come to my house and suitcases on the doorstep very often and wondered what I did and where I went. I breathed a prayer of thanks for God's kindness at another opportunity to share.

"I travel across the United States, speaking and teaching women," I ventured.

"That's interesting. On what subject do you speak?" she responded.

Let me confess to you, dear reader, I often respond to that question this way, as I said to her: "I speak to women about prayer and its influence in everyday living." I do this because it can be an open door to an extended conversation. Most people know something about prayer. It worked once again.

Without asking about prayer or what I teach, she said, "Oh, would you pray for me?"

By now, I knew her name. "Janet, I'd be honored. How can I pray for you?"

Her emptiness and thirst came flooding out: "I'm a newlywed. We are quite wealthy. Well," she continued, "I was wealthy when I married! I did not know at the time that I had married a man who is an addictive gambler. He has lost everything I had and has now walked out on our marriage."

My heart sank. That still, small voice had tried to interrupt me six months earlier about her need.

And She Was Thirsty

I'm a list person. Are you? I make my daily list, my weekly list, and my monthly list. I just love lists. I can't live without a list. My husband says that I will be miserable in eternity if I am not able to have a list. Are you like me? At the end of the day as I check off my list, if I've done something that day that was not on my list, I put it on and mark it off. I know you are laughing! I can hear it! Surely there will be a corner in heaven for all of us list makers.

Jesus was also a list maker, but His list only had one thing on it: to do the will of His Father. You never see Him check things off His list because His lifestyle was His list. His whole life was a ministry of interruptions… on His way to the cross.

> *Fixing our eyes on Jesus, the author and*
> *perfecter of faith, who for the joy set before*
> *Him endured the cross.*
>
> —Hebrews 12:2

Take time to read the eighth chapter of Matthew. You will see that on that day of His life, Jesus was interrupted many times. Each interruption met the needs of the people, showed His power, and displayed God's glory. His single purpose was to be about His Father's business. On His list was the cross. On His way to the cross, He just kept stopping along the way, embracing the interruptions, so that He could minister, heal, and offer eternal life. You might think He was collecting an army of ragamuffins, calling them to follow Him from trees, dinner tables, tax offices, beds of prostitution, fishing boats, sickbeds, hillside coliseums of thousands, beachside breakfast feasts, fish-and-bread picnics, and even a Roman cross.

Jesus's ministry was one of interruptions based on a heavenly agenda. Can you catch the vision of a life of interruptions with a heavenly purpose? (*Lord, teach me to joyfully accept Your interruptions to my list. Oops! I mean YOUR list.*)

I receive a daily devotional online from writer/missionary Elisabeth Elliot. I loved discovering that Elisabeth is a list maker. This one hit home. Hear her words:

> I am a list-maker. Every day I make a list of what I must do. I have an engagement calendar and an engagement book. I have a grocery list on the wall beside the refrigerator, last year's Christmas list in this year's engagement book (so I won't duplicate gifts), a master list for packing my suitcase (so I won't forget anything), a prayer list (a daily one and a special one for each day of the week), and several others. Recently a wholly unexpected minor operation badly interrupted my list of things to be done that week. But because God is my Sovereign Lord, I was not worried. He manages perfectly, day and night, year in and year out. The movement of the stars, the wheeling of the planets, the staggering coordination of events that goes on the molecular level in order to hold things together. There is no doubt that he can manage the timing of my days and weeks, so I pray *Thy list, not mine, be done.*

My life was interrupted a long time ago during a fall weekend youth retreat when I was a youth director in a local church. At the close of the campfire service, I was making my way back to my cabin when one of the young people came to tell me that Julie needed me back at the campfire. I found her in tears—unable to talk. I held her, waiting for her to compose herself. Finally, she was able to tell me that she was not a Christian. People just thought she was because of her parents' leadership roles in the church. We talked until the wee hours. Then she prayed to receive Christ, and I'll never forget the look of joy that gleamed from her face. The presence of Christ was all over her. I suggested she make her commitment known to the church family the next Sunday. She promised.

That Sunday morning, I prayed for the young people as many of them made their way to the altar in response to the retreat weekend. Julie was not one of them.

Weeks passed. The youth group was full of excitement in the Wednesday night Bible study, and the interest and attendance grew continuously. I stayed busy with all the preparations—but then finally realized that Julie was not ever there. I asked one of the teens about her absence.

"Haven't you heard? Since the retreat, she has gone back with the old crowd. She's really gone back to her old lifestyle."

My heart sank. I had not been in touch with her since the retreat, and when I called to check on her, she was rude and unwilling to talk to me. I struggled to think of a way to connect with her, not knowing that a crisis would soon bring us together.

As I prayed asking God for direction, the thought came to me that I should ask her to babysit on Wednesday nights once in a while, so my children's bed-time schedule wouldn't be continually interrupted. That opened a door to get her back into my life.

One Sunday afternoon, when one of our children was ill and I needed a sitter, I called her. She answered the phone, but said she could not come because she was too sick. She did sound terrible. I asked what was wrong, and her response was such that she thought she might die. I told her I would be there in five minutes.

I left quickly, leaving my minister husband with our two small children. She met me outside her house and got in my car, and we drove around while she told a most sordid story describing her young life. Her story literally took my breath away. There was not much left that she had not experienced. I offered a listening heart and my friendship, wondering what on earth I could do to make a difference.

As I drove back home, my heart ached for her. Her words haunt me still. She said, "People in the church always say, 'Call if you need me.' You're the first one to ever come."

The journey lasted well over a year. It was a risk. Sometimes while she was babysitting my children, I would return home to find things—and people— in my home that I would not otherwise accept. The situation called for more prayer! More trusting the Father that He was indeed leading in this troubled relationship. The phone rang often that year, many times late in the night, and I knew it would be her, sobbing about what she had just done and wanting to know if God could forgive her. She had enormous anger at the church because she had seen firsthand that people could not accept her "messy spirituality," as Mike Yaconelli's book title states.

During that year, Bob and I wrote a youth musical called *Now Hear It Again*, and much of the text for the musical came from my friendship with this young girl. In one part, the question is asked: "Are you often lonely...even in a crowd?" Because I could see the depth of her loneliness, these words haunted my heart. She needed someone with a listening heart whom she could trust to show her God's love.

The time for our fall youth revival arrived. The speaker was a man from the West Coast who was having a great impact on high school students all across the Midwest. We made arrangements for him to deal with the issue of drugs at assemblies in both high schools in our city. Many were praying that Julie would hear and respond. His message struck her so hard that she literally ran from the assembly in her high school!

I had not been asking her to come to church, but because the youth choir was to premiere our new musical, I took a chance and invited her to the opening night of the youth revival. After the musical and the message, the altar call was given. I looked everywhere for her and was disappointed...until from nowhere, she came running down the aisle. She grabbed me saying, "You wrote those words about me, didn't you?" Through our tears,

I affirmed her words, saying to her: "I have prayed for you to come home to the Father, and I am glad He used these words and the message to bring you home."

And She Was Thirsty

An interruption? Yes. God is looking for women who will invest their lives in children and teenagers who are in trouble—offering to them the gift of grace that is freely given to us and should be freely shared. Most teenagers need some *significant other* beyond parents to help them walk the tough years of growing up. They need a coach, a teacher, a mentor, an older sister in Christ, a guidance counselor, a neighbor, or a grand-mother. What an opportunity to *splash the living water* in your world!

One verse that intrigues me in my study of the story of the woman at the well is John 4:27: *"At this point His disciples came, and they were amazed that He had been speaking with a woman."* Why were they so sur-prised? Jesus was just being Himself, taking advantage of the interruption as He rested by the well. Even though men didn't speak to women in public during that time, Jesus had shown His purpose was to break down those kinds of walls.

Ask God to place His Spirit on your interruptions, and the world will marvel at the people and places He uses to interrupt you. Ask God daily to make you obedient and to clothe you with His Spirit, and you will be astounded to find these holy interruptions so close at hand.

During one of my seminars, a woman spoke up and said, "After I heard you speak a year ago, I told my husband on the way home in the car, 'that may work for Esther Burroughs, but it sure won't work for me.'"

Then she told me this story: Her family had moved to a new community where her husband was to pastor. They quickly discovered the community was heavily inundated by one particular faith that some considered to be a cult, and the school system struggled with faith issues. She shared how she had prayed for a ministry in her children's school system. When she attended a PTA meeting, the principal asked her to consider serving on a committee to set policies. What great timing in her life.

She told the women in my seminar that she had asked God for opportunities to splash, and she found them everywhere. She started a catering business part-time, and she brought food daily to a movie set in the film industry. God showed her opportunity after opportunity to splash the living water as she met physical needs with the food she had prepared each day for the actors and the production staff.

She was having a dynamic impact on the film industry by splashing the living water through her food service. She asked the seminar group to pray that God would keep her obedient and available. In answer to a woman's prayers, God provided ordinary situations in which she could splash.

These encounters are real! You have thirsty women in your community. Follow Jesus by looking for interruptions, and realize that they can be *life-giving encounters.*

During my early growing-up years, my parents, having five children and living on a preacher's salary, took in boarders (room renters) to help financially. I remember different ones; they stayed in one of the bedrooms. That meant the siblings had to share bedrooms—a very common experience in those days. Most of the boarders ate with our family, but if they wished, my folks provided a small hot plate for them to fix meals in their room. I don't know how, but my mother knew they were thirsty.

I do not remember this practice being disruptive to our family. In fact, it felt like extended family and that was just what it was. What a powerful parenting example that was to teach children that the home is used to splash the love of Christ! Consider using your homes for some type of personal evangelism through small-group Bible study for neighbors and friends from your workplace. I believe the lost art of hospitality is a missed opportunity to share Christ and be an example to our children. Every missionary who came to town ate a meal in our home! My parents made me into a global citizen before I could possibly know its impact on my life.

Bobbie Pinson, a pastor's wife, is a living example of using the home to splash the living water. I heard her husband, Dr. Bill Pinson, tell about a time that he served as a pastor, and his wife, Bobbie, used their home for evangelism. For instance, whenever they moved into a new neighborhood, after getting settled, Bobbie would canvass the neighborhood, knocking on the doors of these new neighbors—introducing herself and asking if there were children in the home. She would tell them that she would be beginning a Saturday morning children's club this week, that included the telling of Bible stories and providing games, crafts, and refreshments, and that she would like to invite their children to come and be a part of this activity for *free*. Well, what mother in her right mind would *not* accept free childcare on a Saturday morning! The neighbors sent the children …and they were thirsty.

Phyllis Harbaugh and her pastor husband, Herb, use Halloween to share Christ. It is a big event in their northern community. One year, Phyllis not only gave treats to the children, but she also invited the parents in their home for hot chocolate and popcorn. This gave her a chance to meet her neighbors, and she shared a gospel tract in the popcorn bag. She has led many of her neighbors to Christ.

They Must Have Been Thirsty

On my grandfather's farm, I remember the big salt blocks that the cattle came to in the afternoon. I watched as they quietly stood licking the salt. Pretty soon they moved from the salt block to the watering trough, drinking in their fill of water to quench their salt-induced thirst.

Matthew 5:13 in *The Message* translation states it clearly: *"Let me tell you why you are here. You're here to be salt-seasoning that brings out the God-flavors of this earth. If you lose your saltiness, how will people taste godliness?"*

In today's self-absorbed culture, you and I must live in such a way that our daily encounters develop in others a thirst to find the well of living water.

Splashed and Splashing

1. Have you ever been ***thirsty?*** Have you experienced ***spiritual thirst?*** Explain.
2. Who offered you a drink of water?
3. What is it in your life today that keeps you from heavenly interruptions and splashing the living water?
4. Make a list of potential opportunities in your neighborhood/workplace.
5. Choose one or two opportunities, and put these on your prayer list. Look for interruptions to share Christ. Bathe this list in prayer.

More Splashing
Study Matthew 25:31–46.

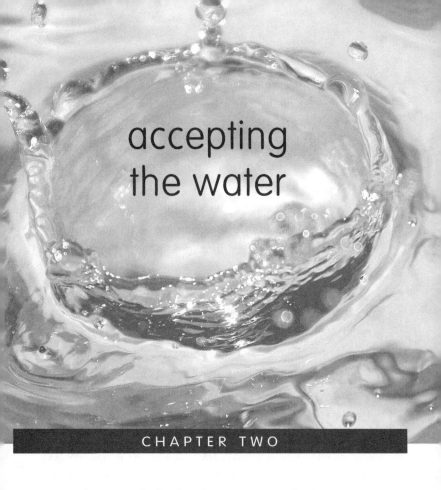

accepting
the water

In order to splash the living water of Christ onto others, you must first let Jesus fill you to the brim with Himself. If your heart is filled with the things Christ gives to His beloved, you will naturally overflow to others you meet. I remember a time God brought my life to a halt so that He could refill my thirsty heart with His living water.

My husband and I were on our way to San Francisco to be involved in a missions conference at Golden Gate

Baptist Theological Seminary. Bob was to lead the music, and I was to be the missions speaker for the conference. We had looked forward to this experience. On our way, we stopped by Vail, Colorado, to visit our son, David, who was involved in a marvelous ministry to the International World-Class Ski Championship.

While there, David convinced his dad and me that we should learn to ski and that he could teach us quickly, so we could be on the slopes in no time, sailing through the powdered snow just like the pros. I looked over the skiing crowd at Vail, and I wanted to ski just to get to wear the brightly colored ski outfits! Besides, I had been an athlete in college days—maybe I *could* do this. The key words in that last sentence are *had been!* I, with a bit of hesitancy, said, "I'm not sure I can do this, David. I'm too old!" He, of course, stretched the truth and said I wasn't, so Bob and I decided to give it a try.

What happened next should have been my first clue that skiing was not what it's cracked up to be. As we ventured out on the bunny slopes, David said to us, "First, you have to learn to get up. The hardest part about skiing is learning to get up." I thought to myself, *That's also the hardest part about life, too—just getting up after life knocks you down.* (Or is it? Perhaps if we, as busy, driven women, could learn to take some down time—sit still, enjoy some quiet time, and **center the heart**—we would handle the *getting up* part of life more efficiently.)

Bob and I did quite well at first. I had fallen a few times on the beginner's bunny slope, but was getting the hang of it. Then David suggested that we take the ski lift to the next level. I'm really slow, I guess, or I would have realized what this second level meant!

For you nonskiers, let me point out that you must be able to get on and off the ski lift at just the right moment, because other persons behind you will be getting off the ski lift whether you are out of their way or not.

I got off—but it might be more accurate to say I fell off. I managed to quickly drag myself out of the way at just the right moment before being run over by four skis!

I got to my feet by using the skill David had taught me and moved down the ski path a bit to wait for Bob and David. I quickly noticed how steep the mountain was...and how close I was to the edge of the ski path. I said to myself, *Get closer inside, Esther, or you'll go down the side of this mountain and make a new ski trail.* While attempting this corrective maneuver, I fell. I don't remember whether it was the pain I felt or the sight of the glove on my right hand turned the wrong way that alarmed me most, but I immediately cried out, "I've broken my arm!" My words echoed across the Rockies.

Bob raced to me while David went to call the ski patrol. The patrol arrived, looked at my situation, and decided to ski me down the mountain on a stretcher sled and take me to the emergency room of the local hospital. I later learned that as they skied me down the hill, I was sometimes being pulled and sometimes being lifted in the air!

I can still recall two things: 1) I was wrapped tightly in the sleigh stretcher but no one thought to take off my ski mask. I thought I might suffocate before I got down the mountain. 2) Every so often, my son, who was skiing right beside the stretcher, would lean over, look in, and say, "You're going to make it, Mom." How often women desire to hear someone say those exact words, ***You're going to make it.***

Once we arrived in the emergency room, the hospital staff confirmed what I expected but dreaded to hear. They told me I had a clean break in the middle of my upper right arm, and in addition, I had a crushed right shoulder bone. I had done it up! Since this kind of accident does not require surgery, they immediately placed me in a Velcro wrap that held my right arm tightly in place at my waist, to speed the healing process. They put no cast on my arm.

Not only had I shattered my bone, but I could also sense a shattered trip to San Francisco—a trip that was very important to me. "Can I still go to San Francisco... please?" I asked the doctor. He simply replied, "No!" In fact, he sent me back to Atlanta. Bob went on to the missions conference while I returned home, in great pain and under great stress.

My recovery time from the ski accident became one of the richest times in my life. Because of this accident, I had to cancel all my speaking engagements for about six weeks. Each day of recovery was spent in front of a fresh fire blazing in the fireplace, Bible open in my lap. I began reclaiming the promises of God given to me throughout my life. Many times I had longed for and dreamed of a six-week vacation package! Who wouldn't? Many times I had longed to be at home sitting in front of the fire—reading, taking care of my heart and soul—with time off the road. I would have settled for just a day or two rather than six weeks!

I had no idea that God would teach me so much during the next few weeks about my worth as His daughter. I had been busy speaking all over the country, dealing with a heavy travel schedule, and not allowing myself much down time. I loved everything I was being allowed to do. Before the ski accident, if you had asked me about my relationship with God I would have said, "It couldn't be better." Was I in for a big surprise! The accident caused more than just my arm to be examined. It allowed me to see the X-ray of my heart before God. Spending hours in Bible study provided a *Holy Spirit X-ray* of my condition before the Father. It was as if the Father said, "Esther, I don't want your busy schedule; I want your adoration. I want the little girl in you to relax in our friendship."

I now recognize the difference between dutifully having a quiet time and expectantly knowing the Father waits to meet me. He desires that we meet Him. I began to learn about balance—taking in and giving out, caring for body and soul, and learning to play hard and to work hard. I began to learn some very specific things about who I am because of Jesus. And my thirsty heart began to be filled again.

Accept Who You Are in Christ

When I speak to women's groups about being a woman of God, I often deal with the issue of self-esteem. I tell them that Psalm 139 is my "horrible, very bad, no-good day" fix. Look at it with me. I invite you to accept your God-given **designer look.** The psalmist says that our Master Designer knew all about us from the time we were formed in our mother's womb, and even before we were born, He knew all the days of our individual lives. No wonder the psalmist cries out, *"I am fearfully and wonderfully made"* (Psalm 139:14). *The Message* translation of Psalm 139:13–17 says it this way:

> *Oh yes, you shaped me first inside, then out;*
> *you formed me in my mother's womb.*
> *I thank you, High God—you're breathtaking!*
> *Body and soul, I am marvelously made!*
> *I worship in adoration—what a creation!*
> *You know me inside and out,*
> *you know every bone in my body;*
> *You know exactly how I was made, bit by bit,*
> *how I was sculpted from nothing into*
> *   something.*
> *Like an open book, you watched me grow*
> *   from conception to birth;*
> *all the stages of my life were spread out*
> *   before you,*
> *The days of my life all prepared*
> *before I'd even lived one day.*
> *Your thoughts—how rare, how beautiful!*
> *God, I'll never comprehend them!*
> —Psalm 139:13–17 *(The Message)*

The psalmist leads us to acknowledge that we can't begin to number the precious thoughts God has about us—they number more than the grains of sand. You will never find this kind of guarantee on the designer dress label on the clothes you wear. God says, *The life you wear (live) is so precious to Me; My thoughts about you outnumber the sand.* Wow! Only God can keep this promise! Think of this promise the next time you are stuck in traffic or in a long grocery line, running your fourth carpool of the day, or finding you are late for your beauty appointment. Put verses 5, 6, and 17 on a card and keep the card on the sun visor in your car. Then, whenever necessary, pull down the visor and bask in these words:

> *You have enclosed me behind and before,*
> *And laid Your hand upon me.*
> *Such knowledge is too wonderful for me;*
> *It is too high, I cannot attain to it.*
> *How precious also are Your thoughts to me,*
> * O God!*
> *How vast is the sum of them!*
> —Psalm 139:5–6,17 (NASB)

Our culture screams to you: Do this! Wear this! Try this! Our Heavenly Father gently whispers, *My daughter, be still! Hush! Listen! Rest in Me. Praise Me, for you are fearfully and wonderfully made.*

Some years ago, I heard on a talk show an interview with the young actor whom you might remember as the title character from the TV series *Webster*. The host asked, "You are just like Gary Coleman. Even your shows are alike. What do you say to that?" Webster's answer was marvelous. "No sir," he said, "You've got that wrong, cause he's he and I's me."

I laughed, embarrassed in the realization that in God's kingdom, comparisons are not allowed. Women make a terrible mistake comparing ourselves to others. God does not measure us against each other. We do that. His standard is far higher. Holy God measures each of us against His Son, Jesus. That should change your focus. God will not ask us if we wear specific clothing labels. He will want to know if we are clothed in Christ Jesus.

The biblical truth is that each woman of God is uniquely created and gifted for the purpose of bringing glory to God. This sets us apart from the world. We don't take our standard from the world's fashion design-ers. We take our standard from the Master Designer! He not only designs us, but also equips us with all spiritual gifts in Christ Jesus in order to be able to live like He calls us to live!

My desire for you is that this message be placed into your heart. You will never again have to look at a label in your dress as a measure of success or esteem. You will always wear God's label—***Chosen in Christ Jesus***—in your heart. Let's look at some of the things that become true about you when you are chosen in Christ Jesus.

In their book, *Captivating*, John and Stasi Eldredge say, "Reading George MacDonald several years ago, I came across an astounding thought. You've probably heard that there is in every human heart a place that God alone can fill....But what the old poet was saying was that there is *also* in God's heart a place that you alone can fill. 'It follows that there is a chamber in God Himself into which none can enter but one, the individual.' You. You are meant to fill a place in the heart of God no one and nothing else can fill. Whoa. He longs for *you*."

You Are Blessed

You can choose to replace your self-esteem with *Christ Esteem* by choosing to accept the truth of Ephesians 1, that we are blessed in Christ! And what a blessing that is! Paul shows us how Jesus, the Messiah, is tirelessly bringing everything and everyone together. He has included us in this plan and chooses to work in and through us. Because we know God's plan of reconciliation, it is urgent that we accept ourselves and see ourselves as part of His plan, which is to bring the world to Himself. We must not waste time comparing our gifts; we must use our gifts to further the kingdom. Embrace Paul's words to the Ephesian Christians as your own.

Have you ever said to someone, "Good morning, how are you?" and received the answer, "I'm blessed"?

It makes me smile. Paul says we have every blessing in Christ Jesus. Our position in Christ ensures this because before He laid down the earth's foundations, He had us in mind and chose us to be the focus of His love. Read the first chapter of Ephesians and underline each time it says "in Christ" or "in Him." The blessings don't just begin when we reach heaven; they are also for life today.

I love to be around the person who lives joyfully, praising God for his every blessing. God chooses to bless His family. Og Mandino says. "Your life can be changed if you choose to live, in love, by four stated rules." One important rule is to count your blessings. I tried it. As I traveled the 45-minute drive to work, I listed my blessings aloud. It does change your attitude. Most often I broke out in song. Your position in Christ assures that you are blessed today and forever.

You Are Chosen

If you are or have been married, recall your engagement day. As love was expressed, you were asked to share a life together. You were chosen. You were to be given a new name, a new direction in life.

God made it easy for all of us to understand that we are "chosen in Christ" by showing us His chosen Son. God announced at the beginning of Jesus's ministry, *"This is My beloved Son, in whom I am well pleased"* (Matthew 3:17). Jesus was the focus of God's delight. So are you! Don't we often find ourselves running and doing, and isn't it related to acceptance from others? Our focus is not right! It is God's acceptance, which we already have in our salvation, that matters. We often carry out this insecurity in the body of Christ, the very place where the whole body has acceptance and grace in Christ...or that is how it should be. Brennan Manning suggests that most of us in the church are "impostors." We keep trying to prove our worth with activity, rather than resting in the relationship. I love Scripture where God speaks to His chosen people.

> *"I have called you by name; You are Mine!"*
> —Isaiah 43:1

> *But the Lord has taken you and brought you*
> *out of the iron furnace, from Egypt, to be*
> *a people for His own possession, as today.*
> —Deuteronomy 4:20

> *You are a chosen race, a royal priesthood,*
> *a holy nation, a people for God's own*
> *possession.*
> —1 Peter 2:9

Perhaps our culture's struggle with esteem is an issue of ownership. We are not our own. John 1:11 says, *"He came to His own* [possession]*, and those who were His own did not receive Him."* First Corinthians 6:19–20 says, *"Do you not know...you are not your own? For you have been bought with a price: therefore glorify God in your body."*

Don't ever forget. You are His possession! We are women living as cherished, chosen possessions of God. YES!

You Are Holy

Holiness is not a reward to be grasped; it is a state of becoming, a relationship to be lived. To be *holy* means we are set apart. You are set apart *by* Christ and *for* Christ. As a bride, you are set apart for your husband, just as the church, the bride of Christ, is set apart for Christ, the bridegroom.

For too long, I thought holy living was only for Bible times or ministers or missionaries. Perhaps I saw lives given to holiness and made the false assumption that I could not live that way, when in reality, that is exactly what God calls and empowers me to do. The prophet Isaiah prophesied about Christ in chapter 35, verse 8: *"A highway will be there, a roadway, and it will be called the Highway of Holiness. The unclean will not travel on it, but it will be for him who walks that way."* What way? The holy way!

You Are Blameless

Have you ever accused your children and then had them respond, "It's not my fault; I'm not to blame" or "Don't blame me, I didn't do it"? After a particularly hard day with her three-year-old, my daughter felt she'd been unfair with her oldest child. Waking her up the next morning, she asked Anna to forgive her.

"What for?"

"I was unkind to you yesterday, and I'm so sorry."

Anna looked at her mother and said, "Forget ye'terday Mommy."

Blame means to condemn or to be at fault. **Blameless**, then, is to be without blame or fault because someone else took all the blame. Jesus took all the blame for our sins and cried out from the cross, *"It is finished!"* (John 19:30). When Jesus finished His work, we were made clean...not guilty...blameless.

You and I stand guilty, full of sin, and yet we need not carry the guilt. Could it be that many Christians live joyless lives because they continue to carry the blame and guilt that God has already banished from His sight? God never reminds us of what He has already forgiven. We, too, may "forget ye'terday."

You Are Adopted

Several years ago in a worship service, the Todd Watson family was called to the altar to present their newly adopted two-year-old son. After the pastor's prayer of dedication, Candy, the new mom, went back to her place in the choir as Todd carried their son to the nursery. It was a touching moment, as little Anthony began waving to his mother and called out, "Bye, Mommy!" I cried. How quickly Anthony had bonded in love with his new mother. How pleased our heavenly Father is when we, as adopted sons and daughters, cry out, "Daddy."

The Holy Spirit is the witness of your adoption into Christ's family when you receive Christ as your personal Savior. The Holy Spirit is the guarantee of things to come in your life as a Christian. I'm told that you cannot undo adoption papers, and the same is true of your salvation experience. The Holy Spirit indwells you and He never leaves. Salvation is for eternity.

You Are Forgiven

We live in the grace of His forgiveness; He took our sins and dropped all charges against us! All my life I have heard that Jesus died for me. If I were the only person on earth, He would have died for me. But consider this truth as well. Jesus died in an act of self-denial and in obedience to God His Father, and you and I are the beneficiaries of that act of grace so that we may extend the gift of grace to others. His obedience is our Amazing Grace!

His sacrifice on the cross was for the forgiveness of our sin. But even though He forgets our sin, He will never forget us. Isaiah 49:15–16 says, *"Can a woman forget her nursing child and have no compassion on the son of her womb? Even these may forget, but I will not forget you. Behold, I have inscribed you on the palms of My hands."* Never forget your name is written on His hands.

A college retreat I attended had the theme of God's forgiveness. The retreat had been a powerful experience. In the last session, the speaker gave each person a scrap of paper and invited us to write on that paper the one thing or issue that we continually begged God to forgive. We were then instructed to get alone to think and write that one issue. While we wrote, a large wooden cross was brought in, placed on the floor in the middle of the room, and surrounded by hammers and nails. Students were invited to nail their issue to the cross, as music softly played. Slowly...reverently...the pounding began, pulsing the message of forgiveness. Tears streamed as hammers pounded the cross: ***Forgiven!***

> *And you, being dead in your trespasses*
> *and the uncircumcision of your flesh, He has*
> *made alive together with Him, having forgiven*
> *you all trespasses,* ***having wiped out the***
> ***handwriting of requirements that was***
> ***against us****, which was contrary to us.*
> *And* ***He has taken it out of the way,***
> ***having nailed it to the cross****.*
>
> —Colossians 2:13–14 NKJV

I'll never forget what happened next. Crying shifted to singing and dancing with great abandon. This type of celebration worship might not be done in your church, but it has been happening since the time of King David. Forgiven! Then we must also forgive.

You Are Redeemed

We are also redeemed by His love. Redeemed, according to the dictionary, means to pay a ransom or to buy back. Sin separated us from Christ, and He paid an awful price to buy us back. We are God's by creation and because sin came into the world, God chose to bring us back to Himself through His Son's death on the cross, which cried out for all the world the good news: **Redeemed!** We are twice His! We are His in creation and His in redemption.

We live in the shadow of the cross. How can we not accept His acceptance of us?

> The price was high.
> The cross was heavy.
> The debt was paid.
> The sinner is forgiven!

In Luke 21:15, Jesus was teaching the disciples the dangers of the life ahead of them and told them to not ever prepare to defend themselves. *"For I will give you utterance* [a mouth] *and wisdom which none of your opponents will be able to resist or refute."* As for wisdom, James 1:5 tells us where to go: *"But if any of you lack wisdom, let him ask of God, who gives to all generously and without reproach, and it will be given to him."* In Ephesians 1:7, Paul says that in Christ we have all these gifts—redemption, forgiveness, wisdom— *"according to the riches of His grace which He lavished on us"* [made abundant toward us]. I believe His wisdom and insight are given to us when we meet Him in the Word. From the God-breathed Word, we are encouraged, instructed, corrected and inspired.

O how I love Your law! It is my meditation
    all the day.
Your commandments make me wiser than
    my enemies,
For they are ever mine.
I have more insight than all my teachers,
For Your testimonies are my meditation.
Your word is a lamp to my feet
And a light to my path.

—Psalm 119:97–99,105

You Are Joint Heirs with Christ

I had two small shadowboxes in our family room. One was for the Milligan side of our family and the other was for the Burroughs side. I have a hankie and wedding ring from both our grandmothers, pins from both mothers, and a ring and hankie that belonged to me, so these boxes contain three generations of treasures. My will states that one box is for my daughter and the other for my son—each an heir; but to be honest, the boxes went to their new destinations before our last move. Even though I have already given them to my children, I can still enjoy them when I'm visiting in their homes.

Speaking of wills, have you written your will? If you haven't, you should—immediately, if not sooner! We write a will so our heirs—those who will inherit our estate—will know what is given to them by birthright.

Do you own something that once belonged to a grandmother? Do you own something that once belonged to only Christ? We believers do. We are joint heirs with Christ by birthright. Our inheritance is in Christ Jesus. Remember this: ***Whatever is His is yours.*** Yet consider this haunting question: ***Is what's yours His?*** Does your relationship with Christ draw you to be His totally? We are rich in Christ Jesus with a richness the world cannot possibly provide through any estate or will.

Enjoy Your Position in Christ!

Everything that is given to us from our Father is to be accepted by us for the purpose of giving praise and glory to the Father. This answers the question: How shall I live? We live not by just surviving in the culture—but by choosing to live in the culture, giving praise to the Father through our lives, acting like daughters of the King. That, dear reader, is true kingdom living!

Don't you feel rich—knowing that you are blessed, chosen, holy, blameless, adopted, forgiven, redeemed, and joint heirs with Christ? Often teachers put stamps of approval on student's papers: GOOD—EXCELLENT. The Father's heart stamps His love for you with these words from Ephesians 1:6 (NKJV): *"accepted in the Beloved"!* Women, enjoy your position in Christ!

The ski accident mentioned earlier taught me some valuable lessons and gave me new insight.

***What I did not want:* Brokenness.** My broken right arm forced rest. My life literally ground to a halt! The forced rest period initially seemed to be a time of brokenness in my life. I discovered that brokenness is often a time of healing. I discovered that I was *running* when God was asking me to *rest* in order to *refresh*, *renew*, and *revitalize* my spiritual energy. I discovered I was dashing here and there, helping the airlines stay in business, and working hard to earn acceptance, when He had already offered me His acceptance.

What I did not know: **Dependence.** I did not know how much a broken right arm would slow me down. Without use of it, I was almost powerless. Slowing down in any area of life tends to make us feel as if we are losing power. I thought I could do it all, in spite of my broken right arm. But my husband literally became my right arm. He did almost everything for me during that six-week period. At that time, he was freelancing, and his calendar was clear to be with me most of the time during that healing process. He would not only fix my meals but also cut up the items on my plate, and sometimes, early in the recovery process, feed me! I learned I was completely dependent on him and had to trust him for every need.

What I needed more of: **Humor.** I realized through this accident experience that humor has a valuable place in our lives—we tend to be too serious about life. Everyone needs to laugh more! The accident changed all that for us! How could I not laugh at myself without makeup! I'm at the age at which makeup is more important than my dress. When my husband would take the hair dryer and go one direction, and the hairbrush would go in another direction, I would end up having a wild hairdo. We both would laugh. You should have seen me trying to dress. I could not put on clothing by myself and had to rely on Bob. My first postaccident attempt at putting on a pair of panty hose would have been a video classic, to be sure (but thankfully there are no pictures)! We laughed again and again.

The first time I spoke publicly after the accident, my arm was still in a sling. I discovered I couldn't talk without my hands. It was a terrifying experience for me. We laughed about that in the car on the way home, as Bob shared that he could see and feel me losing my train of thought, needing my hands to describe my words.

During those healing days, I could do so little for myself. Things that once seemed so serious and important became events for laughter. The world went right on by...not missing me in the slightest way. That fact spoke volumes to my heart. I had to laugh about all the running in my life: No one even noticed when I had to stop.

Well, God finally got my attention so I could learn intimacy in quietness and sufficiency in Him. I came before Him day after day in childlike faith, and He whispered exactly what He wanted me to hear and understand.

The second time I spoke after the accident, a fellow staff member from the place where I worked flew back on the same plane. After hearing me speak, he gave me a good critique: "You need to use more humor in your speaking; you take yourself too seriously." He then complimented the humor I had used. That conversation turned out to be a teachable moment for me. I've been having the time of my life ever since. I had thought all along that what was important was what *others* thought of me. I have now come to peace in believing that what really matters is what *God* thinks of me. I relax more now and let laughter come through my childlike faith.

What I did not realize: **My thirst** I was dry and didn't know it. My thirst for spiritual matters and rest before the Lord was deep. I would bask for hours in Bible study and prayer. I found myself centering internally on things spiritual and found myself thinking less and less about the busy schedule—all my activities and future events. Time flew! I would be called to eat, and thinking it was about time for lunch, I would be surprised to discover it was time for supper. Those days, I had rested in the Lord all day, and He had ministered to me through His Word, through great books, and through inspirational messages and articles.

What I needed to learn: **Humility.** One evening, I was called to supper. The dinner table was set with our best china, crystal, and silver. Bob was serving a lavish dinner he had prepared. He had even ordered flowers for the occasion. It was a special time, for sure! How humbling...to be served, and not be able to serve in return.

I was powerless. I was shown that we humans are dependent on each other to sustain life; we thrive in community. I am still somewhat struggling with the realization that I cannot do everything by myself, and that I need other people in my life to help me with my journey. Rather than self-esteem, I am learning the Lord is my only esteem.

You Don't Have to Be Alone

My husband has the gift of mercy. (I don't! I've even taken a spiritual gifts test twice to see if I did—cheated the second time and still failed.) His gift touched me deeply and taught me the powerful work of God's love—that unconditional love—for me. God takes us at any stage and rearranges our agenda for His agenda. He then empowers us with His Holy Spirit, doing for us what we can't do for ourselves.

In one of my previous books, *Empowered,* I told how I was trying to get my sweat pants off at the end of a day during the ski accident recovery period. Bob was kneeling down and untying my tennis shoes. I was tugging away at the sweat pants, saying to him, "I can do this by myself."

He looked up at me and gently said, "But you don't have to."

Later that evening, when we retired, he fell asleep as quickly as his head hit the pillow. Not me. Late into the night, Bob's words washed over me with the truth of God's message for me, *But you don't have to.* We no longer need to say, "How shall I survive?" You can say,

"I will live...choosing God's esteem and the power of Christ through the Holy Spirit."

Women of God, claim your birthright, which will enable you to live in the power of Almighty God, who created you in His image, and allow you to be your true self, gifted for celebration in the body of Christ to bring honor and glory to God. It's not about you. It is about Him! It is a joyful task!

Chuck Swindoll tells a story of the time his children had a tree house in their backyard. On the door of the tree house, the children posted these rules:

1. Nobody act **big.**
2. Nobody act **small.**
3. Everybody act **medium.**

I can still hear Chuck laughing as he told it. The children were right! **Act medium.** Just be who you are in Christ Jesus!

> *"In a word, what I'm saying is, Grow up.*
> *You're kingdom subjects. Now live like it.*
> *Live out your God-created identity.*
> *Live generously and graciously toward others,*
> *the way God lives toward you."*
> —Matthew 5:48 (*The Message*)

Splashed and Splashing

1. Name the things in your life that you are trying to do all by yourself.
2. List the things you now choose to **surrender** to the Lord.
3. Whom are you choosing to become in Christ Jesus?

More Splashing

Read:

- *Gift from the Sea,* by Anne Morrow Lindbergh (New York: Pantheon, 1992).
- *Freedom of Simplicity,* by Richard Foster (New York: Harper Collins, 1998).

keep coming, keep drinking

Do you ever feel ***thirsty and dry***? When you are spiritually dry and thirsty, where do you go for refreshment? God continually invites us to keep coming and keep drinking of the living water...keep coming and keep drinking...keep coming and keep drinking—to keep our spiritual thirst satisfied.

One night when I had the wonderful privilege of reading bedtime stories to my granddaughter, I received a special blessing. After I finished "just one more" of

Anna's favorites, I tucked her in, and we said prayers. As I was leaving the room, she said softly, "Nana, could you stay just long enough for me to tell you how much I love you?" I leaned back down toward her and thought about staying forever! She then reached up and put her little hands on my face, smiled softly, and said, "Oh Nana, I could never get done telling you how much I love you!"

Women, that is a God story. He never gets done telling us how much He loves us. He never gets done giving to us—filling us up with His love. We need Him every day.

Choosing to Take Time

Robert Boyd Munger states the same idea in his wonderful little book titled, *My Heart—Christ's Home*. Munger urges the Christian to view the heart as a house for Jesus. The young man in his book goes from room to room, walking with Jesus to see what He desires in each area.

First the family room is visited. It has a quiet warm intimate atmosphere. Jesus likes it. It has a fireplace, sofa, overstuffed chairs, and bookcase. Munger has Jesus speak: "Indeed, this is a delightful room. Let's come here often. I will be here every morning early. Meet Me here, and we will start the day together." Morning by morning, the young man and Jesus meet together. Their relationship deepens.

After a while, the young man is beginning to feel the pressures of his many responsibilities. Little by little, he begins to shorten his time with Jesus. Soon, he misses a day...and then another.

One morning, rushing down the steps in a hurry for an important appointment, he sees Jesus sitting by the fire. Suddenly, it comes to him: *He's my guest. I invited Him into my heart! He has come as my Savior and Friend...to live with me. Yet, here I am neglecting Him.* In dismay, the host stops, turns, and hesitantly goes in. With downcast glance, he says, "Master, I'm sorry! Have you been here every morning?"

"Yes," Jesus says. "I told you I would be here to meet with you."

The young man is even more ashamed!

Jesus says to him, "The trouble is that you have been thinking of the quiet time of Bible study and prayer as a means for your own spiritual growth. This is true, but you have forgotten that this time means something to Me, also. Remember, I love you. At a great cost, I have redeemed you. I value your fellowship. Just to have you look up into My face warms My heart. So don't neglect this hour if only for My sake. Whether or not you want to be with Me, remember I want to be with you. I really love you."

I cannot tell you what an impact that story has had on my life. The Lord Himself desires me just to look into His face. I remember those words as I come into His presence daily. He is already there when I get to my quiet time place. He can't wait to be with me...to show me Himself and His truth. He's anxious to hear my petitions, so He can share His words with me. He has already prepared the lesson He will show me that day through His Word. Not only that, but His life is the empowering force in my life.

Create a Sanctuary

> *Now he's using you, fitting you in brick by*
> *brick, stone by stone, with Christ Jesus as the*
> *cornerstone that holds all the parts together.*
> *We see it taking shape day after day—a holy*
> *temple built by God, all of us built into it,*
> *a temple in which God is quite at home.*
> —Ephesians 2:20–22 (*The Message*)

My quiet time place draws me. When I'm on the road speaking, I miss my quiet place as much as anything in my life. I take familiar things with me to help recreate my place. Early in the morning some time back, I was sitting in that blue chair in my quiet place at home when my husband, dressed for his workday, came down the stairs and walked over to my chair. Referring to an upcoming trip I had planned, he said, "I'll really miss you when you're not in that chair." A tender moment it was. His words and their meaning touched me. Friends, my husband could not miss me near as much as God misses me when I fail to meet Him each day.

Let me share a secret: Your quiet time place ***draws*** you. This place begins to look like you and is marked by your habits. My marks are on mine: coffee stains, lists, tears, crumpled tissues, ink marks, song notes still in the air, and even fuzzy carpet knee prints. Seriously! I can see those fuzz marks now as I sit at my computer. *The Message* translation is right: *"We see it taking shape day after day—a holy temple built by God, all of us built into it, a temple in which God is quite at home."*

Here's the rest of the secret: Eventually, His marks are there, too! And you begin to look more like Him. Your heart begins to look like His home, and your life takes His shape as you take on the characteristics of Christ. The reason for being faithful to this relationship is simple: The soul needs nurture. In his book, *My Utmost for His Highest,* Oswald Chambers asks very hard questions: Is the Son of God living in the Father's house—in me? Is the King at home in my life?

The ultimate sanctuary is not a place. It is a person. I am the castle in which He can live—His kingdom in me...on this earth.

Accept the Invitation to Receive

Along with the offer of daily presence, Jesus extends many other wonderful invitations to us. For one thing, He invites us to receive His never-ending supply of living water. Imagine Him personally extending to you the following life-changing invitation:

> *Jesus stood and cried out, saying, "If anyone
> is thirsty, let him come to Me and drink. He
> who believes in Me, as the Scripture said,
> 'From his innermost being will flow rivers of
> living water.'"*
>
> —John 7:37–38

Another offer is found in Matthew 5: *"Blessed are those
who hunger and thirst for righteousness, for they shall
be satisfied"* (Matthew 5:6). This might be translated in
this way: "Healthy are those who have a good appetite
for God."

It would delight the Father for us to sing with the
psalmist, *"As the deer pants for the water brooks, so my
soul pants for You, O God"* (Psalm 42:1).

What an invitation God offers us! "Let him keep coming and keep drinking, keep coming, keep drinking,
keep coming, keep drinking." The supply never runs
out—never ends. This promise has a lifetime guarantee,
and it is yours for the taking. Women know about
running out of everything: time, paper, patience, towels,
energy, money—just everything. That is one reason this
never-ending supply is so...so inviting...so exciting!
What an invitation! Life-giving water—and the very
presence of Christ invites you and me to partake freely.
There is an underlying principle in this invitation. That
principle is this:

- We are invited to take from His supply.
- We are invited to share with others from our
  supply.

Accept the Invitation to Reflect

As we come to Him and drink fully, we begin to overflow and splash on those around us. It is only as we come into His presence and receive His rich supply that we have anything to give. Consider this truth from 2 Corinthians:

> *But we all, with unveiled face, beholding as in a mirror the glory of the Lord, are being transformed into the same image from glory to glory, just as from the Lord, the Spirit.*
> —2 Corinthians 3:18

When we choose to be in His presence daily, an exchange takes place. We are being transformed more into His likeness as the Word of God corrects, refines, and refreshes our daily lives. It is in His presence that our heart and souls are fed. Confronted by the Spirit's conviction, truth is revealed, worship begins, and nurturing happens —Father and daughter confide, confess, and celebrate.

As you and I meet the Father, our lives become like a mirror that reflects His love. It reflects from Him in us to others. We can always know when a woman has been in the presence of Christ. We can feel it, sense it, and, I believe, see it. She reflects Him.

Accept the Invitation to Abide

John 15 is the wonderful Bible passage that invites us to abide in Christ as He abides in us. The study is about the vine and branch relationship. When the branch is not connected to the vine, it dies from lack of nurturing. The farmer cuts it off, because with no connection, it cannot possibly bear fruit. "To make a home within" is a good definition of abiding. Apart from abiding in Christ, having an intimate relationship with Christ, we cannot live a Spirit-directed life.

In knowing His love in our lives, we become His love to the world. So many of us search through religious fads, experiences, and material things, all the while really thirsting to experience perfect love. While they are frantically seeking, God Himself is seeking them—just to be able to express to them His love. Those who know Him must abide in Him so that we can splash His living water to the desperately needy. If we do not abide, we ourselves become thirsty and disconnected. Do you suppose it is the frantic pace of our culture that robs us of His presence, the very essence of empowerment, stolen by our own neglect? We allow ourselves to be robbed of His quiet rest, robbed of the mutual abiding, the ultimate power for life.

We need to abide in His care.

Accept the Invitation to Discover Purpose

The desire of God's heart is for His people to accept His love. Scripture reveals that God has always been calling His people to Himself because He is a calling God, a seeking God, a shepherd—looking after the lambs and calling each one by name. He has a purpose for each of us. Consider the following people He called for His purpose.

God called Abraham to Himself—to father a nation.
"Now the LORD said to Abram, 'Go forth from your country, and from your relatives and from your father's house, to the land which I will show you; and I will make you a great nation, and I will bless you'" (Genesis 12:1–2). God called with a purpose.

God called Moses to Himself—to deliver the nation.
"Therefore, come now, and I will send you to Pharaoh, so that you may bring My people, the sons of Israel, out of Egypt" (Exodus 3:10). God called with a purpose.

God called David to Himself—to shepherd the nation.
"And the LORD said, 'Arise, anoint him; for this is he'" (1 Samuel 16:12). God called with a purpose.

God called Esther to Himself—to save the nation.
"I will go in to the king…and if I perish, I perish" (Esther 4:16). God called with a purpose.

God called Peter to Himself—to build His church.
"And Jesus said to him, 'Blessed are you, Simon Barjona, because flesh and blood did not reveal this to you, but My Father who is in heaven. I also say to you that you are Peter, and upon this rock I will build My church; and the

gates of Hades will not overpower it" (Matthew 16:17–18).
God called with a purpose.

God called Lydia to Himself—to open her home.
"A woman named Lydia, from the city of Thyatira, a seller of purple fabrics, a worshiper of God, was listening; and the Lord opened her heart to respond to the things spoken by Paul" (Acts 16:14). Lydia was the first convert in Europe. God called with a purpose.

God called Mary, Martha, and Lazarus—to share friendship. *"So they made Him a supper there, and Martha was serving; but Lazarus was one of those reclining at the table with Him. Mary then took a pound of very costly perfume of pure nard, and anointed the feet of Jesus and wiped His feet with her hair"* (John 12:2–3). God called with a purpose.

God called Paul to Himself—to invite the outsider in.
"He is a chosen instrument of Mine, to bear My name before the Gentiles and kings and the sons of Israel" (Acts 9:15). God called with a purpose.

God called Jesus to a cross—to offer the world a chance to look into His face and accept His love.
"God is faithful, through whom you were called into fellowship with His Son, Jesus Christ our Lord" (1 Corinthians 1:9). God will never stop calling. God still calls...with a purpose.

A Quiet Time

Let us see how we might look into His face—allowing Him to live His purpose and calling through us. If you are just beginning to take time to meet God daily, consider these suggestions. If you have been meeting Him for a long time, you might still find refreshment or a new direction among these ideas.

Determine a time and place. For years, I thought everyone had to meet God very early in the morning or it didn't work. I'm sure I made folks who were not morning people feel guilty. Ouch! If you are not a morning person, set a time that is right for you. I've heard my husband declare that He believes even God isn't up before 6:00 A.M. It's not the time of day that is critical, but the habit. With the habit established, the time can be found.

Once you know the time that is right for you, determine a place. As you discipline yourself to get into the Word of God, His Word will get into your life, and you will come to cherish the *place* where you meet Him regularly. I feel that the place itself draws you into His presence with joy and expectancy. Make the place your personal sanctuary. A small corner of your favorite room will do...with your favorite chair. Let the place reflect you. Have a basket nearby for your books, pens, and markers. Have a bouquet of daisies, a mug warmer, and, for sure, a throw blanket. Love the place you meet the Father. Love the Father you meet in your place.

Develop a plan. Make a plan. Work the plan. The plan sets your purpose. Without purpose and direction, you will not accomplish your goal of intimacy with the Father, and you will become discouraged. Decide on a minimum time you can spend in your quiet place. If you have young children, your time may be only ten minutes...or less. That's all right. As your life stages change, this amount of time will change also. Your life and work may be such that you can't come into His presence an established amount of time every day. Yet some days, you might find that you have more time. Don't beat yourself up about how much or how little time you can spend. But do get a plan, or it will not happen. As the plan is developing, remember: You are working on a *relationship*...not an *activity*.

Establish a pattern. A novice seamstress must initially follow the pattern directions in order to complete the article she is constructing. As she improves her skills, she may be able to design the pattern herself. As you begin meeting the Father in your time of worship, consider following a pattern of worship. Begin by preparing your heart before the Lord. Follow this by reading an uplifting devotional or a chapter of a book in the Bible. Meditate on Scripture that speaks to you. Then, pray, recording new prayers and thoughts and reviewing the prayer requests already posted in your prayer journal. You will always be adding requests, and you will find yourself dating answered prayers.

Prepare your heart. This may be no more than closing your eyes and inviting God to sit with you. Start each day with words of gratitude and praise. Try reading one psalm daily. The psalms are like hymns and prayers for our lives. Billy Graham even suggested we read from Psalms and Proverbs daily. "The Psalms will tell you how to get along with God, and the Proverbs will tell you how to get along with your fellowman." Music is very helpful; wonderful worship CDs and cassettes are available to lead you into the very presence of God.

Read the Bible. One of the methods God uses to speak to His children is the written Word. Read the Bible devotionally as a storybook. A good study Bible will describe the biblical times, and that information will help you read it as a story. Read the Word of God as if you were in conversation with God. You will find yourself developing a thirst for God's truth.

When His Word speaks to your heart, underline and date that passage. This will become such a joy as days, months, and years later, you recall His promises that have shown His faithfulness to you. I call that walking around in the Word of God.

Meditate on the Scripture. When my son was a little fellow I asked him one day what he was thinking about. "About stuff," was his answer. As adults we need to make the time to think about stuff—creative brooding, in other words. To *meditate* on the Scriptures just means to think about the Scriptures. I have a friend who invites women to read the Bible expectantly. She says to read until God speaks to you in a certain verse. Then, stop and think about that verse. Pray over the verse for yourself or for someone else. You are in the company of the Lord when you meditate on His Word.

> *Let the words of my mouth*
> *and the meditation of my heart*
> *Be acceptable in Your sight,*
> *O LORD, my rock and my Redeemer.*
> —Psalm 19:14

A wonderful way to meditate on God's Word is through praise and worship CDs. You can do this as you carpool...or do the dishes...or even iron! I know my mother prayed Scripture over our clothing as she ironed each piece. She felt she covered her children's clothes in God's Word. Keep three-by-five-inch Scripture cards in your car or purse so you can review during those *high-traffic times* in life.

Pray. Dwight L. Moody said, "Every great work of God began with someone on their knees." I know of no other activity that affects your work more than prayer.

> *"But you, when you pray, go into your inner*
> *room, close your door and pray to your*
> *Father who is in secret, and your Father who*
> *sees what is done in secret will reward you."*
> —Matthew 6:6

Prayer is work and *prayer works.* Listen to what Oswald Chambers says about praying to God in secret: "God is in secret, and He sees us from the secret place; He does not see us as other people see us, or as we see ourselves." (Aren't you glad about that?)

When we live in the secret place, it becomes impossible for us to doubt God. Get into the habit of dealing with God about everything. Chambers also says this about our prayer life: "Unless in the first waking moment of the day, you learn to fling the door wide back and let God into your life, you will work on the wrong level all day, but swing the door wide open and pray to your Father in secret, and every public thing will be stamped with the presence of God." This is a high goal and a wonderful promise.

In my opinion, nothing is more important or has more effect in our lives than our prayers. We must have times of *closet prayer* as well as practice *continual prayer.*

Intercessory prayer is a powerful way to splash the living water. To pray in intercession depends on God's qualities of being all knowing, all powerful, and all present. When we intercede (pray on someone's behalf), we release God's power.

Several years ago, I was one of the speakers for a women's meeting in Illinois. I became reacquainted with a couple that had been students when Bob and I were on the faculty at Samford University in Birmingham, Alabama. They had just been assigned by a mission agency to be missionaries to an unnamed people group. No one was to know the name or location of this people group as protection for the missionaries and their families. They asked if I would pray for them. I was delighted and agreed to do so.

Some months later, I was the worship leader for a large conference. In the opening theme interpretation, flags of all the nations of the world were brought down the aisles one by one and displayed before the audience. Then black flags were presented to the congregation; the black flags represented the people of our world who had limited access to the gospel of Jesus Christ. It was a dramatic moment indeed!

In the conference closing service, I was sitting with my husband in the audience. The minister gave a strong call to missions. He invited the audience to consider prayer as a strategy for unreached groups represented by the black flags, which were still on display. He invited the audience to come forward, receive a card, and, after filling it out, commit to pray for a particular people group. He said that in the next few weeks, the mission agency would send us the name of the people group to which we had been assigned. My heart wanted to respond...but I wanted my husband to go with me. He squeezed my hand. I figured that meant *Yes,* so we moved into the aisle and picked up a card. We filled it out and submitted it.

The following events are indelibly etched in my heart. Several weeks later (I even remember the day of the week; it was a Tuesday), we received a letter from the mission agency providing us the name of the people group for whom we were to pray and information on that group to help direct our prayers. I was so excited! We immediately began to pray for this people group. On Thursday of the same week, I got a letter from the young couple I had met in Illinois. In the letter, they told us what their situation would be, where they would live, and the name of the people group they would serve. It was the very same group...the very same group the agency had given us! Yes! Yes! *Who but God* could orchestrate this in His kingdom work? Many things about their situation are still confidential, but prayer can access a country or language group through the power of the Holy Spirit. Women can have deep spiritual influence in this world through prayer. Chapter 4 will center on the work of prayer in our lives and in our world.

Record your thoughts and prayers. Once you have established your quiet time place, prepared your heart, studied Scripture, and begun to pray, consider praying on paper also—try journaling.

Many resources are available today in bookstores to assist in writing down your thoughts and prayers, but a simple, inexpensive wire-bound notebook will do. As you meet with God, write the Scripture verses that speak to you, and record why a particular Scripture spoke to you and what it said. Stop and pray over the verse. You can pray with your eyes open. If a verse or thought brings a member of your family or another person to your mind, pray the verse for them. Date the notation (I often do this in the margin of my Bible). This type of writing is a way of conversing with God. These jottings can act as your prayer journal where you record your requests and, of course, the answers when they come. This will become a wonderful record of your faith journey. You might prefer to use note cards and then file them. They could be filed by date, topic, or person for whom you prayed.

Read devotional or inspirational books. I like to keep two or three books in my quiet time place so I can pick one up and read a chapter each morning. It may be just the inspiration I need that day for the tasks ahead.

God uses the writings of other people to affirm His truth in our daily lives. Inspirational books are a wonderful way to see the work of God. Every Christian or denominational bookstore has numerous Bible study aids, and most denominations have Bible study outlines that are available for use in personal Bible study. You will quickly discover that the writers of these books and materials are ordinary people—like you and me—on the journey of faith. In my practice of quiet time, I vary devotional helps from time to time, but three things never change. The following three items are always with me during my quiet time:

1. My Bible
2. *My Utmost for His Highest,* by Oswald Chambers
3. A missionary prayer calendar

Oswald Chambers' book, *My Utmost for His Highest,* calls you before God daily. Someone has said in reference to this book, "In most books, you know the author, but with Oswald, you know God." Another devotional classic is *Streams in the Desert,* by Mrs. Charles E. Cowman.

Further Your Spiritual Growth

Did you ever wonder how a Bible teacher knows God's Word so well and why it is so personal to her? The secret lies in her preparation to teach. As she studies, she learns new truth; the Holy Spirit manifests God's Word to her heart and makes it *hers*. She feels ownership in God's promises. That can happen for you also.

Begin with consistent, in-depth Bible study. Real spiritual growth happens when you begin to study the Word of God for yourself. As you dig into the passages, perhaps assisted by commentaries and other biblical helps, you begin to learn to depend on God for direction, rather than depending on a Bible teacher or pastor. The high privilege of personal Bible study will do more to impact your life than any other thing or event. God's Word is a love letter written from Him to you. Cherish it. Study it. Real spiritual growth happens in your life when you study God's Word. It is God breathed... and you can't live, really live, without His breath.

Plan a personal spiritual retreat. When I hear a great Bible teacher share God's Word and His blessings, it develops a thirst in my heart to know God more intimately. I've learned to set aside days for personal spiritual retreats for that very reason.

I know what you are probably thinking. *Sure, Esther! With my hectic schedule and all the responsibilities that are mine, when could I possibly have time to get away on a personal spiritual retreat?* My answer is simply this: Make the time.

A great way to get started would be to schedule a single day for this personal spiritual retreat. Make this time a priority: Put it on the calendar and red flag it.

The ideal situation would be to get away to a nearby retreat center. Many denominations have retreat centers that can be used upon request for a small fee or love gift. When we lived in Atlanta, I was blessed to be just about 45 minutes away from a wonderful monastery. I would often sneak away to this monastery for a few hours, get in one of their small rooms, pray, and study. It was wonderful solitude! Think about it. Can you picture a beach, a park, an assembly, a lake, or even a room at your church that is near your home? Such a place could be accessible to you for a day or a few hours of spiritual retreat. Take your spiritual retreat supplies:

- Your Bible
- Pen or pencil
- Blank notebook
- A workbook Bible study (Something new!)
- Light lunch or snack, if necessary

Now, head out for a wonderful day of quiet before the Father; spend it in the Word and in prayer. I often use a day like this for prayer if I am preparing to speak for a women's meeting. I will take the program of the conference or meeting and pray over every name and event for the weekend—asking for God's anointing on the event.

If you cannot get away for an entire day, schedule half a day. If necessary, you can simply stay right in your own home. Take the phone off the hook, and tell your family to leave a message on the machine because you will not be answering the phone during this time. Two uninterrupted hours can be enough for a good spiritual retreat. I believe women need this time desperately, because we live a life of constant interruptions.

A personal spiritual retreat can take many forms. John Eldredge says, "Young mothers, some days, the most spiritual thing you can do is take a nap." Another idea might be to hide somewhere for two hours with a good book. Just the idea of getting away alone is refreshing. The *getting away* is the secret. This will take real effort because, as women, we always see things that just have to be finished or completed. We crowd out any thought of personal retreat time, which is the very thing we need. OK, so you say you can't possibly get two hours by yourself. Then take one hour, or 45 minutes, or half an hour, but guard the time, whatever the amount, and get started. Make a covenant with yourself.

Jeremiah speaks a strong word to the people of God concerning our intimacy with God:

> *"For my people have committed two evils:*
> *They have forsaken Me, the fountain of*
> *living waters, to hew for themselves cisterns,*
> *broken cisterns that can hold no water."*
> —Jeremiah 2:13

79

Have we, through our busy schedules, forsaken God— the fountain of living waters? Do you ever feel ***thirsty and dry***? When you are spiritually dry and thirsty, where do you go for refreshment? God continually invites us to keep coming and keep drinking of the living water... keep coming and keep drinking...keep coming and keep drinking—to keep our spiritual thirst satisfied.

Splashed and Splashing

1. Describe the place where you meet with God.
2. Does this place draw you to it? If so, how?
3. Perhaps the highest privilege today's woman has is to come into God's presence. How does meeting Him impact your daily life?
4. Do the people you love know that you spend time with God?
5. Describe the marks God is leaving in your life as you meet with Him daily.

More Splashing

Study John 15:1–16, and do the following:

- Find the meaning of the word *abide*.
- Underline each time the words "abide in" appear in John 15.
- Tell how abiding relates to bearing fruit.
- Memorize verse 16.

intimacy through prayer

It was early morning on a fall day in my childhood. I quietly left my bedroom, crossing the hallway to the bathroom to begin making preparations for the day. I heard my father's familiar voice. *Who could he be talking to this early in the morning?* I wondered. An inquisitive child, I followed the sound of his voice. The door stood slightly ajar, and I carefully peeked inside. I have treasured this Kodak moment all of my life. My preacher-daddy was on his knees, his Bible open on his chair, and he was tenderly praying the Psalms back to God. I felt a hushed presence. I could tell my daddy knew to whom he was talking. He was so intimately acquainted with his heavenly Father.

Even as a child, I wanted to know God like that. I stood there, hoping that *presence* would get on me. In the ensuing years, I have discovered I can know God like that—by meeting God like that—daily. By precious example, Daddy taught me to practice the presence of Christ. Prayer is a conversation that never ends. This should thrill women, because we are relational, and in this conversation, the listener friend ***never stops*** listening.

In my family of origin, my siblings and I would quietly laugh, as we talked about prayer and our mother: "If you need prayer, call Neva. She has a direct line to God." The real truth is...each one of us has a direct line to God because of the cross.

On my life journey, I have been privileged to have friends who are real prayer warriors. Thelma Bagby, a missionary who retired after serving 35 years in Brazil, chose to pray for me. She was indeed a woman of prayer. When she prayed, heaven seemed to stand still.

Not only did she pray for me, but she also cared about the results. When I would return home from a speaking engagement, she would call and ask what happened at the meeting! She called me to accountability after every engagement. She would say something like this over the phone: "Where were you on March 25? I must know! What did God do? I was not released from my knees that morning on your behalf until noon. God must have done something awesome." I would check my calendar to remember where I was speaking, and more than once, I have been put in awe at what had occurred in relation to her time of prayer. More than once, I've cried before God at the display of His power and glory because of Thelma's prayers on my behalf and on behalf of the meeting at which I was speaking. What an awesome privilege it is to know you have been prayed for and to know God has answered these prayers—just because an obedient child prayed. Thelma and I became pen pals. When the mail would bring a letter with her familiar handwriting, I would tear it open expectantly. She would speak immediately of Kingdom business with little salutation. Often, her letters were her latest conversations with God and most always included a word for me from that conversation.

I have introduced you to Thelma Bagby because in our correspondence through the years, we have shared our thoughts on prayer with each other. I will now share some of those mutual thoughts with you.

Prayer Is the First Step in Knowing Jesus

It was Saturday night. All was finally quiet when I looked up to see our seven-year-old daughter, Melody, enter the room. By the look on her face, it was more than wanting another drink of water or some other ploy to stay up just a little longer. She crawled into my lap, put her arms around my neck and said these words: "Mommy, I love Jesus, and I want to ask Him into my heart." Those words are a privilege to hear, a privilege to which every parent should look forward. I had prayed that day would come. I got my Bible and began sharing Scriptures with her. I cried for joy as she repeated the words of confession and invited Jesus to come into her heart. We will always remember that next Easter service as our pastor, Dr. Peter James Flamming, said these wonderful words: "I baptize you, my little sister, in the name of the Father, Son, and Holy Spirit."

For everyone, that first step in knowing Jesus is a childlike prayer of confession. What a high privilege and responsibility it is for parents to lead their own children to Christ. The home, even more than the church, should give spiritual instruction. Perhaps the first lesson a child learns in faith is to trust his or her heavenly Father in prayer.

That night as I shared a simple gospel with Melody, I was transported back to my own childhood experience in accepting Christ in my heart. Before I share that with you, let me give you some background on my family.

I have a twin brother. He is six and a half hours older than I am. Yes six and a half hours. We were born back in the dark ages, and the doctor did not even know my mother was expecting twins! I am so glad they found me, because God had a plan for my life.

As a preacher's child, I was raised in a family that observed Sunday as the Sabbath day. On Saturday, my mother made all the preparations for the Sabbath day, which included shoes being shined, clothes being made ready, and, of course, Saturday night bathing. (I still cherish my heritage of Sabbath rituals, even though the rule in our home might seem harsh to some: If you misbehave in church, you get spanked after church. With five children and no nurseries, one or more of us got it every Sunday. I was an adult before I realized that a spanking was not part of the order of worship in a Baptist church.) My siblings and I, as most children those days, had classified clothing: we had *Sunday* clothes and *school* clothes. When our Sunday clothes were too small for our growing bodies, then and only then did they become school clothes.

Now let me tell you about the day I asked Jesus into my heart. It was a Saturday morning and my older sister, Moyra, came into the kitchen, dressed in her Sunday clothes. Mother asked, "Moyra, what are you doing in your Sunday dress?" Moyra responded: "I'm going over to Daddy's study. I'm dressed up today because I'm going to ask Jesus into my heart." Off she went. That was all it took.

I also had been feeling the tug of God's love in my life. I had not as yet been brave enough to respond, but I knew in my heart that I wanted to belong to God's family. When Moyra was out the door, I hurried upstairs, changed from play clothes into my Sunday clothes, and was almost out the back door headed to my Daddy's study when Mother stopped me cold and asked where I was going. I answered much like my sister: "I want to ask Jesus into my heart, too." However, I got a different response from my Mother: I was sent back upstairs and instructed to get back into my play clothes!

I was really ticked off; that was before I knew you could be mad at your mother. I'm sure that according to her mothering experience, my mother thought I was just copying my sister, but my young heart was sincere. I prayed as I changed into my play clothing, "God, hurry and let Sunday get here."

I was the first to arrive in my Sunday school class that morning. As soon as my teacher, Marjorie Gordon, came into the room, I asked her to tell me how I could get Jesus into my heart and be in God's family. She opened her Bible and showed me John 3:16. She led me to read the verse, putting my name in place of *whosoever: "For God so loved the world, that he gave his only begotten Son, that* [if Esther] *believeth in him* [she] *should not perish, but have everlasting life"* (KJV).

I knelt on that cement floor by a little wooden chair and asked God to take away my sin and come into my heart. I could not wait to get home after church that morning so I could announce to my family that I belonged to God's family. I knew so little of what it would come to mean to me—to be in God's family. I knew enough, though, to excitedly tell my family and friends about being in God's family. Prayer is the first step in knowing Jesus.

Prayer Is Conversation between Child and Father

Our Father invites us to pray, and Jesus modeled prayer for us—like a child and a father having ongoing conversations.

When our daughter, Melody, was 18 months old, helping her say her bedtime prayers was a nightly bedtime ritual and one of my special pleasures.

One evening, I asked her if she would like to speak to God. "Yes," she said, bowing her head. She prayed, "Hi, God!" My heart was touched, and I'm sure God's was, too. Jesus Himself called His Father, *Daddy.* I'm grateful for this model of intimacy.

To embrace the truth of Romans 8:34 is to understand prayer: *"Christ Jesus is He who died, yes, rather who was raised, who is at the right hand of God, who also intercedes for us."* Think of it! Get the word picture that is painted here: Jesus stands at God's right hand...with His hands stretched toward us...receiving our prayers...and handing them to God, our Father. That is a guaranteed promise.

If that is not enough for you, read Romans 8:26: *"In the same way the Spirit also helps our weakness; for we do not know how to pray as we should, but the Spirit Himself intercedes for us with groanings too deep for words."* So many times as a child of God, I have not been able to get the words past my broken heart, so I would just cry, and Jesus would explain the reason to God. I can just hear Him say, "It's Esther again and her tears are for...."

It was my habit as an adult child to call my parents every Sunday afternoon—just to check on them and to find out what was going on in their lives. It was also a good opportunity to share prayer requests. My burden somehow felt lighter after sharing it with my parents—

knowing full well that they would also pray for me. We have the same privilege with our Heavenly Father. Jesus stands at the right hand of God—waiting for our requests. He gives us permission to make the desires of our hearts known to Him. He invites us into conversation with Him. Remember that in a good conversation, both talking *and listening* take place, and prayer is conversation between child and father.

Prayer Is a Table for Two

"You are hereby invited to...." The dinner invitation has been extended and you can't wait to get there. You are seated around the table with other special guests. You feel honored. Your best friend is also a guest at the table, and afterward you can't wait to tell her about your conversation with the person who sat next to you.

God Himself through Jesus invites us to His table. In Matthew 22:9, Jesus told a parable to show how eager God is to have His table full: *"Go therefore to the main highways, and as many as you find there, invite to the wedding feast."* Acts 2:42 gives us a picture of believers who regularly practiced being at His table physically and prayerfully: *"They were continually devoting themselves to the apostles' teaching and to fellowship, to the breaking of bread and to prayer."*

Yes, God wants His table full, but when you approach God in prayer, the event can become a private dinner for two—you and God—one on one. Perhaps your time of prayer would have more meaning if you envisioned a table for two, a quiet place for private conversation. How intimate. A cherished time.

> *"Behold, I stand at the door and knock;*
> *if anyone hears My voice and opens the door,*
> *I will come in to him and will dine with him,*
> *and he with Me."*
>
> —Revelation 3:20

I wonder how often the Lord sits at the table, waiting for His invited guests to come. Martin Luther said, "Prayer is the occupation of a Christian. As a cobbler makes shoes and as a tailor makes clothes so a Christian should pray. It is the trade of a Christian to pray." Like the church at Pentecost, we are called to continually break bread with the Master and to pray. E. M. Bounds, author of five books on prayer, says: "We should view prayer as constant fellowship, an unbroken audience with the King. We must see the expectation to pray not only as a divine summons but also as a royal invitation to the throne. We have the privilege of an audience with the King of Kings."

I was in grade school when Princess Elizabeth (now Queen Elizabeth) was to visit our city. In preparation for her visit, the teachers instructed the girls how to curtsy before the princess and how to behave in the presence of royalty.

If I were invited today to visit Queen Elizabeth, I would certainly make all the correct preparations. I would even have someone do my hair and help me select my dress.

Upon arrival in London to see her, I would not rush into the castle and into her court yelling, "Hello!" or "Help!"

Think about it. We do that all the time in the presence of the King of kings. Yes, the King is available to help us, but He also longs for our hearts to come into His courts acknowledging His majesty with praise and adoration.

Jesus's words show us that we are expected to pray. Matthew 6:5 begins, *"When you pray"*; Matthew 6:6 starts with *"But you, when you pray"*; Matthew 6:9 says, *"Pray, then, in this way"*; and Luke 11:9, *"So I say to you, ask,… seek,…knock."* Hear the instructions to pray as the King's invitation. The table is set. He waits for the child to join Him at the table. Never be hurried out of your prayer time. Prayer is a table for two—you and God.

Prayer Is Giving God Access to Your Needs

Your prayer life reveals what you believe about God. Jeremiah speaks about the restoration of God's people:

> *Thus says the LORD who made the earth, the LORD who formed it to establish it, the LORD is His name, "Call to Me and I will answer you, and I will tell you great and mighty things, which you do not know."*
>
> —Jeremiah 33:2–3

A story is told about when author and Bible teacher F. B. Meyer was asked to speak to passengers on board ship. An agnostic listened to Meyer's message about answered prayer and told a friend, "I don't believe a word of it."

Later that same day, Meyer was to speak to another group of passengers. The agnostic decided to attend, but before he went to the meeting, he happened to put two oranges in his pocket. On his way, he passed an elderly woman who was fast asleep in her deck chair. Her arms were outstretched, and her hands were wide open. As a joke, he put the two oranges in her palms. After the meeting, he saw the woman happily eating one of the pieces of fruit.

"You seem to be enjoying that orange," he remarked with a smile. "Yes, sir," she replied, "my Father is very good to me." "What do you mean?" pressed the agnostic. She explained: "I have been seasick for days. I was asking God somehow to send me an orange. I fell asleep while I was praying. When I awoke, I found He had sent me not only one but two oranges!" The agnostic was amazed by the unexpected confirmation of Meyer's talk on answered prayer. Later, he put his trust in Christ. The elderly woman asked, and God used an unsuspecting person to deliver His answer.

In John 14, Jesus invites us to use His name when we pray:

> *"Truly, truly, I say to you, he who believes in Me, the works that I do, he will do also; and greater works than these he will do; because I go to the Father. Whatever you ask in My name, that will I do, so that the Father may*

> *be glorified in the Son. If you ask Me anything*
> *in My name, I will do it."*
>
> —John 14:12–14

He has given us His name…use it in prayer!

My mother was a woman of prayer. Nothing in her life was too big or too little for God. I can remember thinking that my mother could take a nickel and, through prayer, increase its purchasing power to that of a dime. She was a women of strong resolve—telling God her every need. She was a woman of simple childlike faith. When she prayed, she expected God to work. She took God at His Word, often praying Scripture. Simply acting out her faith, she prayed. She told me she prayed while she ironed. Imagine wearing clothes that had been covered in prayer. What great covering!

In the summer of 1996, four hard years after being diagnosed with Alzheimer's, my mother died. Following the memorial service, my father asked me if I would like to have her prayer journals. I was so pleased. I had seen my mother keep these dime-store journaling notebooks with her Bible. It took months before my heart was ready to read her prayer journals. Reading them felt invasive and yet empowering when I saw her commitment to letting God know her needs. Finally, during the week between Christmas and New Year's Day, I took the time to get by myself and read these journals. It was a humbling and inspirational experience.

I found my name written many times relating to family, selling homes and moving, grandchildren, college, and travel—every little issue that life brings. I saw the names of my brothers and sisters and the issues that related to their lives. Grandchildren problems were taken to the Father daily. She prayed for the church family, for her neighbors and friends, for financial and medical issues, for her own needs. I found the names of some of those boarders that stayed with us. Entries were dated as she prayed for their salvation and dated again when and if they came to know Christ.

Mother listed her prayer requests on the left side of the page; on the right side, she often dated the answered requests—I could tell the dating was done at a different time from the prayer request because the ink color was different. During her latter days, even affected by her deadly disease, she was still making entries in her prayer journal. The journal must have been a place of safety for her when Alzheimer's was cruelly taking her life. I was overwhelmed as I noted that on many pages, she listed the request on the left and on the right side, just wrote "Thank you, thank you" by each request...as though in expectancy that the Father would answer her requests. What a walk of faith she lived! I learned from my parents to pray specifically, not generally.

Prayer is giving God access to your needs.

Prayer Releases the Power of God

When speaking in a women's meeting in Oklahoma, I shared how my husband and I had prayed for some 20 years for the mates God would provide our children.

(I often talk about my children in meetings and elsewhere, as most women do.) Our son met and married a young woman who had been born and raised in South Africa by missionary parents. I was telling the audience that day how grateful I was that God had led our son to Colleen and how grateful I was for her parents and for the community of missionaries who helped raise Colleen. I said, "All these years as I have daily prayed for missionaries and their children, I had no idea that God was preparing Colleen for David." The women warmed to my words, because every mother is concerned for the marriages of their children.

My intent in telling the story was to remind the women we can pray for our missionaries, with the awesome knowledge that when we pray, God's power is released to do His work. What I did not know was that a missionary from southern and eastern Africa was present in the audience! After the meeting, this missionary, Barbara Schleiff, came to me and handed me a child's blanket. She said, "As children, Colleen and my son were very good friends." She continued, laughing, "I picked Colleen for my daughter-in-law, but since you won, I brought you Colleen's 'blankie' that she gave my son as she boarded a plane to furlough in the US." What a thrill for me—to meet one of the women who had loved and helped raise Colleen on the mission field. I was looking into the face of an answered prayer. That's awesome! Women, when we pray, God's power is released.

In 2 Corinthians 1:20 we read, *"For as many as are the promises of God, in Him they are yes."* We pray, knowing God's faithfulness in the Word. Proof of His promises go on and on.

I heard Dr. Helen Roseveare share the following experience from her work in the Inland Mission in Zaire, Africa. Dr. Roseveare was called out in the middle of the night to deliver a premature baby. The mother did not live and left behind, in addition to this preemie, a two-year-old daughter. The doctor asked a helper to bring a hot water bottle for the newborn. She returned and told the doctor that when she put the hot water in the bottle, it burst. Dr Roseveare then assigned that helper the task of keeping the premature baby warm through the night.

The next day in her prayer time, Dr. Roseveare told the children about the premature baby, its sister, and the mother. Ruth, a ten-year-old African child, prayed, "God, send a hot water bottle today. Tomorrow will be too late. We need it today. And while You are at it, God, send a dolly for the baby's sister so she will know You still love her."

Helen thought to herself: *I know I should have faith like that, but how can I! We are in the Congo of Africa. Who would even think to send us a hot water bottle!*

Later that day, a runner came to Dr. Roseveare's office to tell her that a car was at her home. She ran quickly, only to discover the car had already gone—but a box had been left on her doorstep. She gathered the children. This was a special occasion. The children jumped for joy when Dr. Roseveare pulled a brightly colored vest from the big box. They loved the candy she pulled out next, but they were not excited about the bars of soap! Next, to the doctor's amazement, she felt something familiar and found a hot water bottle in the bottom of the box. When Ruth saw that, she rushed forth and began to tear into the box with Dr. Roseveare, saying, "If He sent this, there must be a doll!" Further digging did indeed bring forth a doll.

I tell this story often, and each time, my heart bows before God in His extravagant love toward us. *Who but God* could have orchestrated those circumstances?

Six months earlier, a Women's Mission Society in London, England, had prayed for the missionary, Dr. Roseveare, and was led to send her a box that included a hot water bottle and a doll. Imagine that! Women on one continent praying and sending supplies—becoming God's answer to prayer on another continent—six months ahead of schedule. That, my friends, is the mighty handiwork of God! Women prayed and God's power was released and splashed on a mission station in the Congo of Africa. Only eternity will reveal the faithful prayers of God's people and how God's power was released to work, changing eternity. Yes, prayer releases the power of God.

Prayer Is the Soul on Its Knees

With all prayer and petition pray at all times in the Spirit.

—Ephesians 6:18

*Seek the L*ORD *and His strength; seek His face continually.*

—Psalm 105:4

Pray without ceasing; in everything give thanks; for this is God's will for you in Christ Jesus.
—1 Thessalonians 5:17–18

Talking to men for God is a great thing, but talking to God for men is greater still. Several sources suggest that to *"pray without ceasing"* means "to pray with the frequency of a hacking cough."

The story is told of a young man visiting in England in the home of the great preacher A. B. Simpson. Coming down the hallway, the guest passed Dr. Simpson's room and saw the minister in his study at his desk. He stopped to politely say good morning when he realized the minister was reading God's Word. Before speaking, he watched quietly as Dr. Simpson closed his Bible and took a globe in his hands.

The great missionary pastor began to pray. The young guest stood still as if on holy ground, not wanting to interrupt. He listened and watched as the pastor held the globe close to his chest and began to pray for the world. As he prayed, tears began to flow and roll down over the nations of the world. The guest stood still in the presence of a soul on its knees before God.

The missionary, Jim Elliot said, "God is on the throne …we are on His footstool…only a knee's worth away."

Prayer is the soul on its knees.

Prayer Is a Direct Line to World Evangelization

While working with a national mission agency, I was invited to speak to a women's mission group in North Carolina. I did not have Nona Bickerstaff's name on my note page and had not even planned on telling her New York City missionary story. Yet it must have been in my heart, because the story rolled forth from my heart. I told the group of her request to the mission agency for funds to be able to extend for another year a college student's two-year term of service.

The student had said, "If the funds are rejected due to other pressing needs, I will stay anyway, because God called me and the need is so great." Living with little or nothing, she continued to serve. It would only take $3,000 to keep the student on the field.

I said to my audience, "How can you and I not give generously to help meet the needs of one who so generously serves in the inner city?"

After my message, I took my seat on the front row. I heard a commotion in the choir loft where the officers of the organization were seated, having just been installed. They were joyfully crying, and celebration was evident. It was not long until the president of the organization, followed by all the officers, circled me with words spoken too quickly and so full of emotion I could barely understand their words. Finally I heard, "We produced and sold a cookbook, and we put the $3,000 we made in sales in savings, and we have been arguing over what to do with the money for three years. Now we know what to do with the money." She wrote a check right on the spot. I hand-delivered it to the president of the mission agency.

Prayer is a direct line to world evangelization.

Prayer Is an Audience of One

I was invited to speak to a church on a Sunday morning. My husband was to lead the music in that service. As we made our way to the platform, the minister said to us, "There is a woman from Russia in our congregation, and she worships a little differently from the way our congregation does. We are not sure what to do with her."

With that information, he left me, and took his seat across the platform. As my minister-husband stood and invited the congregation to sing, it was not long until I noted the woman from Russia. She stood with the congregation. She was not dressed in bright, rich colors as others near her; she appeared to be dressed in brown. She had on a long overcoat, boots, and a babushka covering all but her face. I saw her hands lifted and heard her voice singing, "Alleluia." I knew that word— the same in most languages.

Later in the service, the minister asked the family of God to bow in prayer. I prayed with my eyes open and watched for my sister from Russia. She stood up, moved out into the aisle, got on her knees, and moved to the altar praying, "Alleluia." My heart wept for courage to get on my knees and crawl to the altar to pray. I was not sure I could speak that morning after her sermon to my life. I did my best.

The offering was taken at the close of worship. Once again, I was called to bow before Holy God as I watched this woman stand and reach deep into the pocket of her coat and pull out a hankie. She untied the knot and emptied the contents into the offering plate. My heart observed that prayer is an audience of one.

My childhood Kodak moment of my father praying (mentioned earlier in this chapter) was being revisited. Watching this Russian woman worship etched a similar scene in my heart again many years later—different persons, different place, different time, but same story.

Prayer is heaven touching earth. We come week after week to worship in freedom. How is it possible that in worship, we are so close to His presence…yet so far from His power? Could it be our inability to bow?

During a visit in the home of my parents, who at that time lived in East Texas, we were watching the Olympic Winter Games in Calgary, Canada, and enjoying the beautiful ice skating events. When the American skater Debbie Thomas did not win the gold medal, my father got up, said his good night to us, and made his way to his bedroom. My mother and I stayed until the very end of the skating competition—hoping against hope that the results might change and that Debbie Thomas might be declared winner by default! Finally giving up, I made my way down the hall to the guest room. Passing my parent's bedroom, I saw my father…on his knees at the end of the day…praying to his Heavenly Father. I cried within myself, *Oh God, let my children see me on my knees before You*. I do not desire that my children and grandchildren necessarily see me on my knees for the show, but for the picture that could be ingrained in their minds. I do desire to live in such a way that they sense that I daily bow before God—just like my father. Prayer is an audience of one. Women of God, **pray!**

Splashed and Splashing

1. Write when and where you prayed to receive Jesus and give your heart to Him?
2. Do you talk more **about** God than **to** God?
3. Which of the following best describe(s) your prayer life? Why?
   - ❏ Prayer is the first step to knowing Jesus.
   - ❏ Prayer is the conversation between child and Father.
   - ❏ Prayer is a table for two—you and God.
   - ❏ Prayer is giving God access to your needs.
   - ❏ Prayer releases the power of God.
   - ❏ Prayer is the soul on its knees.
   - ❏ Prayer is a direct line to world evangelization.
   - ❏ Prayer is an audience of one.

More Splashing

Read:

- *Prayer: Finding the Heart's True Home,* by Richard Foster (San Francisco: Harper, 1992).

clothed in the spirit

After a particularly tiring week, and with many children still around her, Mildred McWhorter, a missionary in the inner city of Houston, Texas, was finally saying good-bye for the day. The little boy she was holding in her arms looked up into her eyes and said, "Miss 'Quater, are you God?"

She drew back in surprise as she continued to hold him and said, "Oh, no! I'm not God...but His Son, Jesus, lives my heart."

"No," the little guy insisted, "You are God!"

Taking another deep breath, she said, "Oh, no! I am *not* God, but His Son, Jesus, lives in my heart."

As he pointed to her heart, the little boy insisted again, "Oh no. I can see Him right there."

Imagine living in the power of the Holy Spirit so clearly that a child feels he can see God in your life!

After working 29 years in the inner city, Mildred McWhorter finally retired. But the city of Houston would be forever changed. Mildred won almost every humanitarian award that could be given by that city, but none of the awards mattered to this missionary giant. She chose to live in the inner city—with the people with whom and to whom she ministered all those years.

Paul says, in 2 Corinthians:

> *Are we beginning to commend ourselves again? Or do we need, as some, letters of commendation to you or from you? You are our letter, written in our hearts, known and read by all men; being manifested that you are a letter of Christ, cared for by us, written not with ink but with the Spirit of the living God, not on tablets of stone but on tablets of human hearts. Such confidence we have through Christ toward God. Not that we are adequate in ourselves to consider anything as coming from ourselves, but our adequacy is from God.*

> —2 Corinthians 3:1–5

I'd like to live like that, wouldn't you? *"A letter of Christ...written...with the Spirit of the living God...on tablets of human hearts."*

I was attending a conference in Hawaii several years ago and was in a Bible study on Gideon defeating the Midianite army. When the teacher got to Judges 6:34, my eyes stayed glued on the page. It read, *"So the Spirit of the LORD came upon Gideon; and he blew a trumpet, and the Abiezrites were called together to follow him."* I looked in the margin for a reference dealing with the words "came upon Gideon," and found that it meant "clothed." The most amazing thing about the Word of God is its *freshness* in our lives. I am sure I had read that text before, but that day, it was as if the Holy Spirit highlighted it with a yellow marker. I remember putting a sticky note on the page to remind me to look it up when I got home.

I really loved the concept of the Holy Spirit *clothing* me. I was so excited because I know about women—and clothes. Imagine—being *dressed in the Holy Spirit!* What a clear word picture for us to remember. I knew women would get the concept quickly! Just as we dress ourselves appropriately for the day's activities, envision the Holy Spirit dressing us for the activity He plans for our lives every day.

After that trip, I began looking at the work of the Holy Spirit in God's Word. I read books about the work of the Holy Spirit. I was drawn to this study, and about six months later I understood the reason why, when a mission agency invited me to write a book about the work of the

Holy Spirit in the lives of ordinary people. The Spirit had already begun to teach me about Himself.

The Holy Spirit is a person, the third person of the Triune God. The Bible refers to the Holy Spirit as the Teacher, the Guide, and One who comes along beside us. We cannot see Him, but we can feel and sense the Spirit if we are listening for that still small voice that gives direction, brings correction, and fills us with the fullness of God. A truth about the Holy Spirit is that He indwells you, clothes you in His power, and chooses to go before you, working ahead of you.

God is committed to the task of working in us, developing us, deepening the character traits of His Son in us through the Holy Spirit until we look like Him. We are not on our own in this process. He has given us the person of the Holy Spirit to see that we become like Him in every way. In fact, the gift of the Holy Spirit was given to us the moment we accepted Jesus as our personal Savior. The question the little boy asked Mildred McWhorter was thought provoking. You see, he had seen the reflection of Christ in "Miss 'Quater," as he called her, and he sensed the Spirit of God in her—she was a *living letter.*

What is a great witness? When I consider that word, I picture a Mildred McWhorter—I think of a woman full of faith and the power of the Holy Spirit. Ephesians 5:18 says, *"be filled with the Spirit."* That literally translates, "be being filled." The great preacher Dwight L. Moody is reported to have said, "We need the continuous filling of the Holy Spirit—because we leak!" I would like to add to that, "and we splash."

Clothed in the Spirit

The Daily Presence of the Spirit

In Ephesians 1, we read these words: *"And you also were included in Christ when you heard the word of truth, the gospel of your salvation. Having believed, you were marked in him with a seal, the promised Holy Spirit, who is a deposit guaranteeing our inheritance until the redemption of those who are God's possession—to the praise of his glory"* (Ephesians 1:13–14 NIV).

We should be as intimately acquainted with the person of the Holy Spirit as the disciples were acquainted with Jesus. Everywhere they went with Him, they felt and experienced His presence. As you and I live out our daily lives, we do so with the presence of the Holy Spirit indwelling us. The doctrine of the Trinity teaches us to have faith in the work of the Triune God: God the Father, God the Son, and God the Holy Spirit. I cannot explain the *three-in-one* and *one-in-three* concept of Holy God. But I do know that water is the same compound whether it is in liquid, solid, or gas form. And I do know that I need water in its different forms—liquid, ice, and steam—at different times.

God the Father sent God the Son.
God the Son sent God the Spirit.
God the Spirit sends you and me.

I believe that today's Christians must become intimately acquainted with the third person of the Trinity, the Holy Spirit.

Teaching about the Holy Spirit, I said to an audience on the West Coast, "If you trust the work of only God the Father and God the Son, you have only two-thirds of the power." An older woman responded, "Oh no. You ain't got **no** power!" I stood well corrected that day.

The Person and Presence of the Holy Spirit

Growing up in church, I heard messages about the Holy Ghost. My child's mind conjured up images that I couldn't imagine had anything to do with God, and I was sure I wasn't supposed to believe in ghosts. I was an adult before realizing through study that the Holy Spirit is a person. For you and me to know the reality of the Spirit in our lives, we must look at the person, the presence, the work, the acts, the authority, and the filling of the Holy Spirit to enable us to acknowledge and embrace the power of the Holy Spirit.

When Jesus lived on earth, He ministered through His physical presence. He ministered in all the places where He could physically reach. The person of the Holy Spirit does not have a physical body and is thus free to minister wherever He chooses. You have felt His presence many times. Don't you often walk out of worship saying to yourself, "Wow! We could really feel the Holy Spirit this morning"?

In your own time of worship, often the wind of the Spirit draws you through the refreshment of His Word. I think of the Spirit in terms of the breath of God. An old hymn by Edwin Hatch implores, "Breathe on me, breath of God, until my heart is pure." Amy Grant sings a wonderful Christmas song as a prayer of Mary. The song pleads, "Breath of Heaven, lighten my darkness, pour over me your holiness, for you are holy." This could be your moment-by-moment prayer for the breath of the Spirit to pour over you—and through you.

One of the terms the Bible uses to describe the Holy Spirit is **wind**. In speaking of the new birth, Jesus said to Nicodemus, *"The wind blows where it wishes and you hear the sound of it, but do not know where it comes from and where it is going; so is everyone who is born of the Spirit"* (John 3:8).

The Holy Spirit is the **Sent One.** We do not need to cry for the Heavenly Dove to come among us. The Holy Spirit is already among us! The Holy Spirit is here—now. We did not ask for the Holy Spirit. He is the Sent One. Listen to what Jesus said about the Holy Spirit: *"But I tell you the truth, it is to your advantage that I go away; for if I do not go away, the Helper* [the one called along side to help] *will not come to you; but if I go, I will send Him to you"* (John 16:7).

God the Son sent the Spirit—one member of the Godhead—to work through us. It is through the ministry of the Holy Spirit that every other ministry that God provided and His Son purchased becomes real to us. The Spirit adopts us into the family. He regenerates us and cleanses our lives. He indwells us so we embrace the whole of the Trinity...the Father, the Son, and the Holy Spirit. He teaches us, speaking through His Word. He reveals to us the things of Christ that we cannot see, and that enables us to glorify God. He empowers us by personal relationship, pouring out His power through us.

The Work of the Holy Spirit

When you and I think about a doctor, we immediately know the role that he has. A doctor diagnoses our illnesses, prescribes medicine, and shares medical knowledge. Medically trained, he is charged with administering his medical gift. We may see him in different settings and circumstances, using different parts of his gift as he practices medicine.

The person of the Holy Spirit also has different roles. He is Teacher, Guide, Power, Truth, Helper, and Gift Giver, to name some. One work of the Spirit is to draw persons to Christ.

In Acts 10:1–5, we read the story of Cornelius and his vision, which tells him to send some men to Joppa to bring back a man called Peter. Did you ever wonder why the angel did not tell Cornelius how to be saved? The angel instead told him to send for Peter. The angel did not tell him because the angel could not tell him. The angel did not know salvation. God had to use an instrument that knew salvation. Peter was to be that instrument.

Cornelius sent two of his servants and one of his soldiers to get Peter. About noon the following day, as they were on their journey, Peter went up to the roof to pray. He also had a vision; his was about eating meat that was unclean. While Peter was wondering what the vision meant, the men sent by Cornelius found the house where Peter was staying and called for him. Peter was still thinking about the vision when the Spirit said to him, *"Simon, three men are looking for you. So get up*

*and go downstairs. Do not hesitate to go with them, for
I have sent them"* (Acts 10:19–20 NIV).

How clear the visions must have been to both
Cornelius and Peter because they were both obedient
to the message. And because of this, the Gentiles heard
the gospel. I believe the Holy Spirit speaks this clearly
and specifically in our lives today. Trust the Holy Spirit
to do just that in your life, but remember, your job is
to listen. In your quiet time or in worship, has some
thought nudged your mind and your mind replied with
I can't possibly do that—not now anyway! or *What would
people think or say, if I was obedient to the Spirit's voice?*
Pause to reflect whom you are answering. Is it the
whisper of the Spirit?

The Holy Spirit Precedes Us

A woman in one of my seminars told about her friendship
with a couple in her church and her prayers that they
might come to know Christ. The wife, Penny, responded
first. Then she and Penny continued for a long time
praying for the husband, Jim. Both continued asking him
if he was ready. His response was always the same: "I'm
just not ready quite yet."

Some months later in a special service, the couple
was in attendance. Penny said that during the invitation,
the Holy Spirit whispered to her to go and stand by Jim
and simply say, "Are you ready yet?" That time, he ***was***
ready…and he did accept Christ. His response to her
afterward was this: "I was just praying, 'God, let Penny

come back and get me and take me to the pastor, I'm ready.'" Wow! Trust that the Holy Spirit's work is to precede your work.

I often wonder what would happen if I obeyed immediately each time the Holy Spirit nudged my heart. What might happen in your church if Christians were immediately obedient to the Holy Spirit's voice? We second-guess, pondering where that thought came from, or we decide that we just can't possibly do that today—instead of obeying, in faith, the *whisper* of God's Holy Spirit.

The Holy Spirit Convicts

It is so freeing to me as a child of God to know that I am not responsible for leading someone to Christ! That is the work of the Holy Spirit. If we think **splashing** or **sharing Christ** is much too difficult, we are not trusting the Holy Spirit to work through us, drawing people to Christ.

> ***Splashing is not about scripture memory.***
> ***Splashing is not about doing something.***
> ***Splashing is not about passing or failing.***
>
> ***Splashing is all about relationships.***
> ***Splashing is all about friendship.***
> ***Splashing is all about being His fragrance.***

My dear friend the late Thelma Bagby said, "It's about two people...in love: God and you!"

We are in a relationship with Christ, and talking about that relationship should be the most natural thing to do.

Clothed in the Spirit

I believe women fear sharing Christ partly because they have the mistaken view that *we* are responsible to win that person to Christ. The good news is this: that is the Holy Spirit's work! That is the work He came to do. It is not ours and we can relax in that fact. Our work is to be obedient to share Christ in the naturalness of who we are...with the gifts we have been given. We can tell our story...and share our relationship with another person, but we cannot save them. That is the work of the Holy Spirit.

I was to be in Richmond, Virginia, for several days speaking for several different events. I lived in Atlanta, Georgia, at that time and thought of the state of Virginia as being in the North. I assumed the weather would be cold during the time I was to be there. It was not! In fact, there was a heat wave—in early March. My room was on the front side of the hotel, and the sun poured through the window. I had walked early that morning—not wanting to walk in the hot sun. Back at the hotel, I was ready for that first cup of coffee to enjoy during my quiet time. My mind said, *No...iced coffee would be welcome.*

Writing in my journal that morning, I was fussing about the heat, as I did not have the proper clothing. I was interrupted by a knock on the door, and the maid asked if she might come in to clean the room. "Certainly," I said as I greeted her with a pleasant voice, as if I had not just been complaining to God.

"Are you having a good day?" I inquired.

"Not so good," she responded.

"Is there anything I can do?" I asked.

"Oh, no. Somebody just stole $60 from me, and I say stole 'cause I did not give permission for them to take it."

Immediately, a small voice spoke inside my heart reminding me that I had $60 in my purse. I am not accustomed to giving away money, so I ignored the thought. I asked her a few questions about herself and whether she went to church in the neighborhood, thinking I could get her in touch with a minister who might help her with the money.

"No. Not since I was a child." She continued, "You see my rent money is due. I live in a neighborhood where you have to board up the windows and double lock the doors, and women get abused and robbed all the time. But it's the only place I can afford right now."

She now had my full attention. Just minutes before she walked into my room, I was complaining about the awful heat...in the safety and security of a hotel room. Once again, I offered to help but she insisted there was nothing I could do. That small voice was still whispering to my heart.

I noted her nametag and called her by name, "Patti, did you say you don't go to church anywhere in the community?"

"No. Not since I was a small child."

Bravely, I said, "Patti, has anyone ever told you about Jesus or would you say you are in the process of discovering who He is?"

"No one has ever told me about Him. Can He help?"

While I caught my thoughts, she kept talking. "Will you tell me about Him?"

There I was…Bible in hand…having my quiet time. I stammered out these words: "Well sure, I can tell you about Jesus, but don't you think we should ask your supervisor if we can take the time to talk?" You see Patti was on company time. So was I.

She said, "Oh, my supervisor won't mind. She has already been praying for me."

Wow! Her response should not have surprised me in the least. This was a divine appointment. You can trust that the Holy Spirit is already working ahead of us.

I invited her to sit beside me on the bed, and I showed her several Scriptures from Romans:

For all have sinned and fall short of the glory of God.

—Romans 3:23

But God demonstrates His own love toward us, in that while we were yet sinners, Christ died for us.

—Romans 5:8

For the wages of sin is death, but the free gift of God is eternal life in Christ Jesus our Lord.

—Romans 6:23

> *That if you confess with your mouth Jesus*
> *as Lord, and believe in your heart that God*
> *raised Him from the dead, you will be saved;*
> *for with the heart a person believes, resulting*
> *in righteousness, and with the mouth he*
> *confesses, resulting in salvation.*
> —Romans 10:9–10

She quietly prayed the prayer to invite Christ into her heart. When we finished, she jumped up immediately and said, "I must clean your room!"

"Don't bother," I offered, since I had already made the bed.

"Well, I'll at least do the bathroom." When she walked to the bathroom, you guessed it; my heart knew I was going to give her the $60. I went into my suitcase and got the money, a gospel tract, and a small card and wrote her a note, asking her to read the little tract when she got home that evening. When she finished the bathroom, I gave her the envelope and said, "Patti, will you promise me that you will not open this note until you get home tonight?" She agreed. That felt safe to me.

When she left my room, I realized it was 8:30 in the morning—the exact time my senior adult friends, Ruth Fennell and Ida Richards, always prayed for my daily travel calendar. I loved the truth these godly women knew. Now they are both in the presence of their King. When they prayed, God opened the heavens and brought glory to Himself by working through us. So

I picked up the phone to call my prayer partners, and as I dialed the number, another knock came at the door. Hanging up the phone, I went to the door to find Patti standing there. She said, "I came back to tell you something." I invited her inside. She said, "I feel so clean all over."

"Patti, that is just how you feel when Jesus comes to live in your life. It does feel clean all over."

"Well, there's something else, too."

"What is it?" I asked, wondering what she would say.

"When you read to me from that book…that one," she said, as she pointed to my Bible, "that one over there…I felt something coming from you to me."

What a joy it was to tell her that was the Holy Spirit. And He was God's gift to her, giving her power.

Women, God's Holy Spirit goes before us daily in our lives—empowering us to trust Him to work through our lives. Imagine my joy when Patti shared that her supervisor had already been praying for her. We can trust the Holy Spirit to work in our lives just like He worked in the lives of Cornelius and Peter. The Teacher—the Guide—goes before us in everything we do.

Trust that truth! There is nowhere you can go but that the Holy Spirit is already there. Add this truth to your heart. He, the Holy Spirit, indwells you. He clothes you with Himself, and clothes Himself with you. His holy presence in you can draw people to Christ. He is responsible to draw them to Christ—and sometimes it will be through you.

Pentecost was for you and me as much as it was for the early disciples. The same Holy Spirit comes to us in our salvation…clothing us with Himself.

John 16:8 says, *"And He, when He comes, will convict the world concerning sin and righteousness and judgment."* Aren't you glad you are not in charge of convictions of sin and judgment? The work of the Holy Spirit is to bring the person from death to life. Think back to the day you asked Jesus to come into your heart. Remember the tender voice of the Holy Spirit that drew you into His presence. Remember the Holy Spirit calling you to Christ. Remember the first place you prayed to receive the gift of salvation in your heart.

The Holy Spirit Reveals God's Existence

People often question how a person could come to know God if they have never heard the story. Paul clearly states that they are without excuse:

> *That which is known about God is evident within them; for God made it evident to them. For since the creation of the world His invisible attributes, His eternal power and divine nature, have been clearly seen, being understood through what has been made, so that they are without excuse.*
>
> —Romans 1:19–20

Since the creation of the world, the Spirit of God has been making Himself known to man.

> *God uses nature to reveal Himself.*
> *God uses music to reveal His symphony of grace.*
> *God uses art and literature to show His creativity.*
> *God uses life experiences to reveal His ever-present existence.*
> *God uses people as instruments of His power.*

Part of the work of the Holy Spirit is to reveal the truth of God's very existence.

The Acts of the Holy Spirit

I can't wait for you to see the acts of the Holy Spirit in the book of Acts. For all the Holy Spirit activities described in the book, it could be named *The Acts of the Holy Spirit*. This book has mystery, in the appearing of the Spirit. It has miracles, worked through ordinary disciples, full of the Spirit's power. It has extravagant love, displayed in church sharing. It has extraordinary worship and powerful praying. It has eternal implications for the Gentile nation. It has jail scenes and angel gatekeepers. It has my attention. Nothing can block the power of the Holy Spirit in the acts of the Holy Spirit. Nothing at Pentecost! Nothing now!

I heard a pastor give a great outline for the book of Acts:

Chapter 1: ***The Savior went up.***
Chapter 2: ***The Spirit came down .***
Chapter 3: ***The Saints went out.***

Let's spend some time looking at the first few chapters of Acts.

After the resurrection but before being lifted into heaven, Jesus commanded His disciples *"not to leave Jerusalem, but to wait for what the Father had promised"* (Acts 1:4). They then questioned Him whether this was the time He would restore the kingdom to Israel.

Jesus responded, *"It is not for you to know times or epochs* [God's destined time] *which the Father has fixed by His own authority; but you will receive power when the Holy Spirit has come upon you; and you shall be My witnesses both in Jerusalem, and in all Judea and Samaria, and even to the remotest part of the earth"* (Acts 1:7–8). To be sure they were equipped for His work, He asked them to wait until they were **clothed with the Holy Spirit.** Read Acts 2 to picture the clothing session.

As they waited, they heard something. *"And suddenly there came from heaven a noise like a violent rushing wind, and it filled the whole house where they were sitting"* (Acts 2:2). They heard the rushing wind. Remember that John said we don't know where it (the

Wind of the Spirit) comes from—or where it is going. But they heard it that day! This is one of the ways the Spirit works.

As they waited, they saw something. *"And there appeared to them tongues as of fire distributing them-selves* [being distributed], *and they rested on each one of them"* (Acts 2:3). They saw what appeared to be tongues of fire that sat down on each one of their heads. What a sight that must have been—each one clothed in the fire of the Holy Spirit. No wonder the early church turned the world upside down.

As they waited, they felt something. *"And they were all filled with the Holy Spirit and began to speak with other tongues, as the Spirit was giving them utterance"* (Acts 2:4). They felt the all-consuming power of the Holy Spirit filling them that day, and they each began to speak in tongues. This event was so powerful that the Jews living in Jerusalem gathered when this sound occurred, and they were amazed and marveled. The followers were full of the Holy Spirit. In fact, these Christians were so full of the Holy Spirit's power that some in the observing community thought they were drunk—*"full of sweet wine"* (Acts 2:13). They were acting under the controlling power of the Holy Spirit. This is a good illustration of the Spirit's power being so in control of our walk that we are not even acting like ourselves... we are acting like Him.

After they waited, they said something. Pentecost changed Peter the most. He took the stand, raised his voice, and preached a strong message right from the prophet Joel. When he finished, the people in the crowd were so touched that they asked what they needed to do: *"Now when they heard this, they were pierced to the heart, and said to Peter and the rest of the apostles, 'Brethren, what shall we do?'"* (Acts 2:37). Peter said, *"Repent...be baptized...and you will receive the gift of the Holy Spirit"* (Acts 2:38). Three thousand persons responded that day. Peter preached under the authority and controlling power of the Holy Spirit.

After they waited, they did something. The church responded, as the church always will respond, to the working of the Holy Spirit. *"They were continually devoting themselves to the apostles' teaching and to fellowship, to the breaking of bread and to prayer. Everyone kept feeling a sense of awe; and many wonders and signs were taking place through the apostles"* (Acts 2:42–43).

Not only were wonders and signs taking place, but powerful prayers were being offered and the truth was being spoken with boldness. *"And when they had prayed, the place where they had gathered together was shaken, and they were all filled with the Holy Spirit and began to speak the word of God with boldness"* (Acts 4:31). How long has it been since your place of prayer was shaken? They prayed, and then they spoke boldly the Word of God.

The Authority of the Holy Spirit

A desire of my heart would have been fulfilled if I had met Corrie ten Boom in person. Corrie was a woman who lived in the authority of the Holy Spirit. The closest I ever got to her was visiting her childhood home in Holland, reading her books, and seeing the movie *The Hiding Place*.

After the tour of the ten Boom home several years ago, my friend Jo and I decided to take tea in the little shop across the street from the site. As we sat down, Jo laughingly accused me of standing so close to the sofa in the family room that she guessed I was tempted to sit down on it. She was right. As we walked the cobblestone streets to the church, I said to myself, *maybe she stepped here, and here, and here.* It was a time of remembering what God's Spirit had done in one life that was totally committed to Him.

The story is told that the lives of more than 800 Jewish people were saved because of Corrie ten Boom and her family. I whispered in my own heart, *God, use me like you used Miss Corrie.* I heard one of Corrie's friends tell about the time she visited Manly Beesley in the hospital on one of the occasions before his death. Manley said, "Talking to Corrie was being privy to her conversation with God. She would be talking to you—then look up and talk with God awhile—then turn back and pick back up the conversation with you. She was so intimately acquainted with her heavenly Father that she carried on a running conversation with Him hourly."

During this particular hospital visit, the phone rang, and it was the Billy Graham organization tracking her down to tell her that they would have to stop the movie production of *The Hiding Place* due to lack of funds. Miss Corrie's response was this: "That is no problem. It is God's will for the movie to be made. We are being obedient, so continue with the film."

The voice on the phone said: "We can't. We are out of money."

"That's no problem. My Father owns the cattle on a thousand hills," she said and hung up. It wasn't long until a Texas rancher sold some cattle and sent the money to the Graham organization—designated for this film. Corrie lived in tune with the authority and power of the Holy Spirit.

The Great Commission, as found in Matthew 28, calls us to trust His authority given to us from His command:

> *And Jesus came up and spoke to them, saying, "All authority has been given to Me in heaven and on earth. Go therefore and make disciples of all the nations, baptizing them in the name of the Father and the Son and the Holy Spirit, teaching them to observe all that I commanded you; and lo, I am with you always, even to the end of the age."*
>
> —Matthew 28:18–20

The promised power comes with the presence of the Spirit, *"Lo, I am with you always."* We are able to trust the Holy Spirit when we understand the Holy Spirit is the authority, and He gives us boldness and wisdom.

After Peter's great message in Acts 2, Peter, accompanied by John, offered healing to a lame man in the name of Jesus, then preached a sermon and offered an invitation to repentance. For this they were put in jail overnight. The next day, the rulers, elders, and scribes gathered and questioned them: *"By what power, or in what name, have you done this?"* (Acts 4:7). Peter, *"filled with the Holy Spirit,"* spoke so boldly about Jesus that the listeners were amazed. *"Now as they observed the confidence of Peter and John and understood that they were uneducated and untrained men, they were amazed, and began to recognize them as having been with Jesus"* (Acts 4:13). What a profound testimony! They, through the knowledge of Christ Jesus and the filling of the Holy Spirit, were filled up to all the fullness of God, as described by Paul: *"To know the love of Christ which surpasses knowledge, that you may be filled up to all the fullness of God"* (Ephesians 3:19).

I believe when a woman's life is clothed with the authority of the Holy Spirit, persons in her circles of influence will recognize that she has been with Jesus. You perhaps have been in the presence of such a woman. You feel drawn into her spirit and refreshed by His Spirit in her, and when that happens, God gets the glory. Oh, my sisters in Christ, that is what I desire, and I know you desire in your life: to be filled to all the fullness of Christ—empowered by His Spirit to live boldly daily in all circumstances.

You and I must learn to trust the authority and power of the Holy Spirit in our lives. In Luke 12:11–12, Jesus refers to the Holy Spirit as a teacher. *"When they bring you before the synagogues and the rulers and the authorities, do not worry about how or what you are to speak in your defense, or what you are to say; for the Holy Spirit will teach you in that very hour what you ought to say."*

James 1:5 gives us more encouragement: *"But if any of you lacks wisdom, let him ask of God, who gives to all generously and without reproach, and it will be given to him."*

The Holy Spirit Takes Action

I was flying home from a meeting out West, and just as I got seated on the plane, a young woman named Kim came and sat in the seat beside me. She was expecting a child. She asked me if I was afraid to fly. I told her I was no longer afraid to fly, having experienced almost 3 million flight miles. She told me how frightened she was to fly and that she was on her way to a family funeral. She had never flown before.

I gave her a little pep talk about planes and added that I had prayed that morning, using Psalm 91:11 (my travel verse): *"For He will give His angels charge concerning you, to guard you in all your ways."* She said that she had also prayed that morning, so I asked about her faith background. She shared that she was a Christian, but that her husband was not, and that she was praying for him.

Just before the plane departed, the stewardess, being aware of Kim's fear of flying, checked on her one more time. I assured the stewardess that I would help Kim as the plane took off and that I had prayed for God's protection early that morning. Sara, the stewardess, said, "I do that every morning I fly." Sara then promised she would get right back to Kim after the plane got into the air. Kim's fear was so strong she would not even lean over to look out the window. I thought she might squeeze my hand off as the plane taxied down the runway and lifted into the air.

As we leveled off, Sara came back to offer Kim a soft drink. She thanked me for being willing to help, and I responded that it was my pleasure. I said, "I believe I was to sit by Kim today to show God's care to her as she has a very difficult day ahead getting to the funeral."

Sara said, "I knew you were a Christian. I saw you on this flight yesterday. You had your Bible and a notebook open. I told my cabinmates that you were a Christian speaker. And besides, you had on that same purple dress!" We laughed about the dress, and I confirmed that I was indeed a Christian speaker. I shared with her that Kim told me she was praying for her husband to know Christ.

I thought Sara would jump out of her uniform. She promised again to come back after she served the beverages. When she came back, she told me where she lived, and we discovered her pastor was a friend of mine. Sara turned to Kim and shared how her Bible study group offered her friendship and began to pray for her husband, which eventually led him to Christ. She was so full of excitement as she told Kim her husband's story and promised to pray for Kim's husband—and every person in the first two rows heard about Christ—boldly—from this Christian flight attendant.

Women can trust that the Spirit of God will give them the words to say and the wisdom and tenderness with which to say them.

The Spirit Gives Boldness

I was flying to St. Louis, Missouri, on one of those small planes—not my favorite thing to do. Getting settled, I noticed a tall gentleman wearing a cowboy hat approaching. He sat beside me, tipping his hat as he greeted me. It was a beautiful "cloud day" for flying. As the plane reached its appropriate altitude, he asked, "Do you like the clouds?"

"I certainly do, I think they are one of Gods most beautiful creations," was my response.

"I like them also. Let me ask you, do you believe in angels?"

"Yes, I do. In fact, every time I fly, I claim the protection of angels from Psalm 91."

He smiled.

As we chatted, I had the feeling he knew Jesus.

So I boldly asked him if he did. "Yes, I grew up in a minister's home, but I'm not in church today."

"May I ask why?"

Lowering his head he spoke softly, "I've failed twice in marriage. I am living with this woman, and I really love her, but I can't make that mistake again. You know…you can't go to church when you're living in sin."

I said, "Why not? Everybody else does."

"I guess you're right there, little lady." Yes, he did call me "little lady."

I said, "Why don't you consider going home and honoring your lady friend by asking her to marry you. Confess your sin, and then walk into that church with your heads held high."

Long pause. Tears.

"For months I've been struggling with this and wanting to get back to God and in the church. I don't think it was an accident that I sat by you today."

While waiting for our luggage, he asked, "Lady, do you mind if I give you a hug?" And he did. "I just know God sent you to me today, and I promise you I am going home and get this right before God and walk that gal down the aisle to be my wife and join that church." His smile was as wide as the brim of his hat. A God moment.

Let me tell you, this *little lady* was very happy for boldness in the Spirit's power. Trust the Spirit of God to give you the wisdom, the words, and the tenderness with which to say them.

The Filling of the Holy Spirit

Think back to a recent Bible study or retreat in which you were the leader or teacher. You spent much time in preparation and prayer. When the event or lesson was over, how did you feel? Depleted? You probably physically dropped your shoulders and gave out a deep sigh. Why? You had relied on the power of the Holy Spirit to lead and teach or you might say, you used up your current supply of the Spirit's power. That's why we have to **be being** filled with the Spirit, as D. L. Moody said, "because we leak!" So as you walk from Bible study to church or pack the car after the retreat, you bow again before the Father and breathe in, asking the Holy Spirit to fill you once again.

The power of the Holy Spirit does not leave us, since He indwells us, but we must continually ask for Him to refill us. Just as when a car runs out of gas, it needs to be refilled, so is it when we run low of Spirit power, we need refilling. Nothing is wrong with either "vehicle"; the supply of fuel has just been used up, and refueling is needed!

The filling of the Holy Spirit is a day-by-day, moment-by-moment process. The God of the Old Testament refers often to Israel as a people for His own possession. The filling of the Holy Spirit is for God's people to be possessed by the Holy Spirit's power.

Ephesians 5:18 reads, *"And do not get drunk with wine, for that is dissipation, but be filled with the Spirit."* This literally means **be being filled.** Being filled with the Spirit is a continual process. If we are under the influence of wine, the wine is controlling our behavior, but the drink will wear off after awhile. Paul suggests that we be continually filled...the process of becoming a God-possessed people.

To be filled with the Holy Spirit means to be surrendered to Him—allowing Him to think His thoughts in us and release His power through us. C. S. Lewis, in his book *Mere Christianity,* said the "Holy Spirit empowering us is the difference between paint, which is merely laid on the surface, and a dye or stain, which soaks right through."

So often before or after Jesus would heal or bless someone, the Scriptures record that He went alone to pray, got up early to pray, or prayed all night. Jesus knew the source of the power. Prayer was His way of being refilled.

We are refilled so that we can continue in faith. Colossians 2:6–7 says, *"Therefore as you have received Christ Jesus the Lord, so walk in Him, having been firmly rooted and now being built up in Him and established in your faith, just as you were instructed, and overflowing with gratitude."* Remember, you **continue** in Christ just as you **received** Him as Lord, that is, **in faith.** Your Spirit-filled life is given and maintained by God.

How Can You Be Filled with the Holy Spirit?

Satisfy is defined as, "to fulfill the needs and desire of." As you and I seek after, spend time on, and pursue a right relationship with the Heavenly Father, our needs and desires will be satisfied. In Matthew 5:6, Jesus says, *"Blessed* [healthy] *are those who hunger and thirst for righteousness, for they shall be satisfied."*

We can understand who the Spirit is and how the Spirit works, but we have many questions about how to be filled with the Spirit. It's amazing because we recognize the person whose life is touched by the Holy Spirit, yet we don't see ourselves in that place, simply having the desire to be intimate with Christ. Ask God to put the desire in you to live in the fullness of Christ. Now that is a request He loves to answer.

Start off your pursuit with a clean slate. First John 1:9 states, *"If we confess our sins, He is faithful and righteous to forgive us our sins and to cleanse us from all unrighteousness."*

I've heard preachers say that when they were students in seminary, the great missionary to China, Bertha Smith, when on campus, would walk up to them, point her finger in their faces, and say, "Are you prayed up? Are your sins confessed?" The students were annoyed at her courage but said many ended up on their knees in confession before God.

Bertha Smith says in her writing about the Holy Spirit, "to be filled with the Spirit, you must acknowledge some absolute essentials."

You must give testimony. Share spiritual blessings. Cease to tell, and soon there will be nothing to tell. I believe we miss part of the joy in Christ when we do not tell others what Christ is doing in our lives.

You must constantly remind yourself that you, by nature, are no better than when you weren't saved. *"But we have this treasure in earthen vessels, so that the surpassing greatness of the power will be of God and not from ourselves"* (2 Corinthians 4:7). We hold this treasure in earthen vessels; therefore, we must live our life in the Spirit to bring glory to God. We must form new habits in light of our new position in Christ, including systematic Bible study, prayer, and keeping up-to-date in regard to confession of sins. Confess immediately; this is necessary for the sake of future testimony.

You must keep going on with the Lord daily. A Spirit-filled life is a must to keep walking in Christ. Howard Ramsey, a precious friend and mentor in Christ, says you can never tell another about Christ when there is sin in your own life. It just chokes you. In other words, the Holy Spirit can't flow through you because of this sin. Therefore, confession is necessary and critical to the filling. As in a marriage, when you are upset about something your mate did and you are holding them at a distance, the love can't flow through your anger or hurt. Until you ask or give forgiveness, the love between the two of you is choked and can't get through.

When sin is present in our lives, it is almost as if we hide from intimacy with God. When you get in God's presence, the Holy Spirit reveals truth to us—He may do it through the Scripture, a devotional guide, or a friend—and the convicting presence of the Holy Spirit draws us to confess and be cleansed. As in a good marriage or friendship, when one of the two finally asks for forgiveness, the cleansing power flows freely and draws the two back into intimacy. It happens in everyday life situations. Believe me, confession for me is practiced daily, hourly, even moment by moment.

I had been on the road several days, and my husband, Bob, came to meet me at the airport. This was a real treat, so after we got my luggage, we went out to eat. I became intensely aware that I needed to get home and wash a load of clothes in order to pack for the next day's journey, so I became anxious. The check came, but we just kept sitting there until finally I said, "Let's pay and leave."

He said, "You're paying, aren't you?"

"No, I don't think so."

"Yes, you said you would treat this time."

"No, I didn't," I said.

"Did I?"

"Yes, you did."

"Well, I don't even have my wallet."

"That's some excuse!"

He got up, went to the car to get his wallet, and paid the bill...and we drove home in total silence. Any conversation between us was over. The joy was gone. The delight wasn't there. I was sure he was wrong, and he was as sure I was wrong—all over a few dollars.

When I got home, I began unpacking and repacking my suitcase. Did you know you could make a lot of noise unpacking if you want someone to notice? He ignored me. Climbing into bed later that night, I laid there replaying what had happened. This was not how I'd envisioned our time together. I remembered (that small whisper again) that indeed, I had promised I would pay! Then I could see myself the next day standing up in front of women talking to them about **splashing the living water.** Slowly I moved closer to his side and said I was wrong and asked forgiveness. Oh, yes! Forgiveness...cleansed from unrighteous behavior. You're thinking *that's a small thing.* Have you ever noticed the small things are what catch us off guard and keep us from being the presence of Christ to each other?

To be filled with the Spirit means instant confession, instant obedience. Barbara Schleiff, the missionary I mentioned earlier who had hoped my daughter-in-law would be hers, says, "We must live in instant confession of any sin that the Holy Spirit convicts us of. We must live in instant obedience or we are not filled with the Spirit. Delayed obedience is disobedience."

The filling of the Holy Spirit comes when we desire to be filled, confess our sin, and submit our will to God's will.

Our culture is not comfortable with the word **submit.** Someone has suggested that to submit means to honor another by putting their needs and desires before our own to please Christ. Another meaning of submit is to surrender. Living a Spirit-filled life is to honor Christ by dying to self and putting His desires before our own. Paul, in Romans 12:1, calls us to do that. *"Therefore I urge you, brethren* [sisters], *by the mercies of God, to* *present your bodies a living and holy sacrifice, acceptable* [well pleasing] *to God, which is your spiritual service of worship."* What a powerful statement...called to give my life as a sacrifice in an act of worship to God, submitting to His authority in my life. I believe all submission begins with **the fear of the Lord,** surrendering to the lordship of Jesus Christ.

Oswald Chambers says it very clearly: "The one and only characteristic of the Holy Ghost in a man is a strong family-likeness to Jesus Christ, and freedom from everything that is unlike Him."

John the Baptist said of his relationship to Jesus as he introduced Him to the crowds, *"He must increase, but I must decrease"* (John 3:30). John did not confuse his leadership role. His role was to prepare the people for Jesus. Gordon MacDonald, in his book *Ordering Your Private World,* said of John, "If there was a moment when the crowd's praise became thunderous, the voice of God from within was even louder." MacDonald says that voice spoke more convincingly because John had first ordered his inner world out in the desert. Listening to that inner voice of the Spirit orders our private world and gives focus to our call as Christians. Proverbs 4:23 admonishes, *"Watch over your heart with all diligence, for from it flow the springs of life."*

Our submission comes from that quiet place where our lives are ordered in His will. Out of the quiet order, we receive **the being filled**, **the being clothed** by the Holy Spirit. Submission—like confession—is daily, moment by moment, dying to self, **letting Him clothe**

you in the Holy Spirit. No wonder the little boy asked "Miss 'Quater" if she was God; he saw a life clothed with the Holy Spirit.

I was teaching several years ago at a conference center in New Mexico. I had taught about the work of the Holy Spirit. The women became very excited about the idea of ***being clothed in the Spirit.*** As the week came to an end, I made my way back to the hotel. When I stepped into my room, I found a note under the door. I sat down to read it. It was one of those notes that become a blessing to your life. I was very touched and humbled that God chose to use me in this woman's life. I looked for her address on the envelope so I could write and thank her for her encouragement. I found no address but on the flap of the envelope were these words: "I know you're not God, but you sure are wearing His clothes." My heart cried out audibly, "No! Not me!" Oh my...but, Yes! Yes! Every child of God is clothed in the presence and power of the Holy Spirit!

Splashed and Splashing

1. Can you recognize the work of the Holy Spirit in your life? Give examples.
2. How have you seen God work in the life of a person who does not know Christ?
3. Describe a person you know who is clothed in the power of the Holy Spirit.

4. List some Holy Spirit characteristics in that person's life.
5. Read 1 Corinthians 12. List the various gifts of the Spirit.
6. Describe your gift. How can you use it in the body of Christ?

More Splashing

Read:

- *The Mystery of the Holy Spirit,* by R. C. Sproul (Carol Stream, IL: Tyndale House, 1994).
- *Renewing Your Spiritual Passion,* by Gordon MacDonald (Nashville: Thomas Nelson, 1989).

the wellspring of family worship

We always sat on the first pew—piano side—in my growing-up church. I am sure the four of us sat there so both our parents could watch us carefully and discipline us when necessary. With four small children, no nursery, and our minister-father on the platform, Mother always sat in the middle of the four children. At that time, she had one three-year-old, twin two-year-olds, and one one-year-old...and that's the truth! Only preacher kids could understand the look in the eyes of their daddy from his chair on the pulpit platform. It was nearly always a "spanking look." With four children, one or two of us got it almost every Sunday! I remember it like it was yesterday. Following big church, we walked home. Well, to be honest, we walked everywhere in those days. The parsonage, the house provided for the minister and his family, was on the same property as the church, and only about 50 steps away. The walk home was quiet, and you can be sure the child expecting the *rod* was the quietest. The wooden sidewalk from the house to behind the shed was well worn on any given Sunday. Before he administered the belt, my father would tell us that this would hurt him more than it did us. That speech did not make sense to me—until I had children of my own. Even more today, I know how it must grieve our Heavenly Father when, as His children, we disobey His laws.

I recall a day *all* of us were getting spanked and I cried out, "But I didn't do anything!" My father replied, "Then this is just in case you do." When I remind my parents about this event, they always say, "Look how well you turned out!" So there you have it for raising children in the early days.

Some 14 years later, much to our surprise, our mother went to the hospital with a tummy ache and came home with a baby sister, making five children! Imagine bringing a baby home to four teenage babysitters. What a delight this child was to my parents, and what a precious friend my sister is to me today. I claim the privilege of being the middle child since, as you may recall, my twin brother is six and one-half hours older than me. I was the peacemaker in our family. I am sure that if my siblings were writing this book, they would add that I was also the tattletale. But you must understand, if I was in charge of the peace, I always had to be on the lookout for the troublemakers.

There were rules in my home. Here are just a few of them:

- Children are to be seen and not heard.
- Manners are the rule, not the exception.
- Everyone has chores.
- Respect your elders.
- Sunday is the Lord's Day.
- Always tell the truth.
- Do your best in everything.
- Finish what you start.
- Music lessons are required.
- Grades matter.
- Remember: You are a Milligan!

Family Sabbath

I always felt like that last rule came straight from the mouth of my grandmother. We were taught to live in such away as to bring honor to the family name. That may be old-fashioned, but I choose to believe that a high standard was set for us by our parents and grandparents, and that this standard taught us that the Heavenly Father also wants His children to bring honor to His family name by honoring and obeying Him.

My parent's rule about celebrating Sabbath (Sunday for us) had the most impact on us. The Sabbath was a holy day in my growing-up home. My mother always cooked Sunday dinner on Saturday evening. We cleaned the house on Saturday, so it would be presentable on Sabbath day. Everyone had specific jobs. The reason I remember this is because I was sure my sister always got the easiest job. Even as Mother, in disgust, changed our responsibilities from time to time and switched our chores, I was still certain my sister got the easiest part. I can still taste the dust on that long hardwood rail staircase, which had to be done with a hand cloth, with the understanding that Mother, *the inspector,* would follow up to see if I had done it well. If not, I had to do it over again to please my mother. After all, company just might drop by.

It was a really big event when we got to wear our Sunday clothes, and everything had to be readied on Saturday night. Clothes were pressed and hung, shoes were shined, socks were folded, Bible and offering were laid out—all in preparation for Sabbath morning. Sunday school lessons were prepared on Saturday. Now, that was a task—getting all four children to study their lessons.

These were rituals upon which we counted. I'm sure it must have made Sunday morning a bit easier for our mom, in her efforts to get our large family ready to go to church—on time.

On Saturday night, the dining room table was set with the good dishes—not fine china, mind you, because we didn't have any. We did have good dishes.

We put on a nice tablecloth and the good glassware. As you can tell, we dressed up in all ways for Sunday—not just our clothes, but our home as well. We tried to present the best to the Father. It was not about showing off—it was just the way my family celebrated Sabbath.

As you might now guess, we were not allowed to play on Sabbath day! We were allowed *Sunday toys*—quiet games like puzzles. We could also read good books—like the "Sugar Creek Gang" or "The Hardy Boys" series—or we could read the Bible. As teens, this was difficult because our friends were allowed to play ball or go to the park. For the Milligan children, Sunday was a day for quiet rest in our home.

Family Altar

Each morning during the week when we were called to breakfast, we gathered around the breakfast table, and while the porridge got cold, my father opened his Bible and read the Word of God to us. As a child growing up, it felt like he read *all* of the Old Testament—every day! After Father read, we got down on our knees by our chair, and Father prayed for each one of the children—by name. Then, he prayed for all the missionaries—by name. With the prayer finished, we were then free to eat breakfast. This was known in our home as *family altar*. We did this every morning of our lives—even on Christmas morning! I remember my parents praying for very specific things in our lives—often reminding God about our personal attitudes and behavior. I once heard

Chuck Swindoll say these dynamic words: "Pray over your children, and touch them even as they go out the door to school. You will be giving them a blessing for the day."

In biblical times, parents blessed their children with physical touch and spoken touch—words of affirmation. In Jewish tradition, the father assumed primary responsibility for training the child. The Jewish law states, "It is the duty of every father to train his children in the practice of all the precepts" (Solomon Ganzfried, Hyman E. Goldin, Joseph ben Ephraim, *Code of Jewish Law* [New York: Hebrew Publishing Company, 1963; Code IV, 47]). My parents parented us, basing their care for us on Proverbs 22:6: *"Train up a child in the way he should go, even when he is old he will not depart from it."* To a strict Jew, that meant the way of his father and his father's father. Every Jewish child learned Deuteronomy 4:6–9, and parents taught their children God's law as instructed in Deuteronomy 6:1–7:

> *"So keep and do them* [the commandments of the Lord], *for that is your wisdom and your understanding in the sight of the peoples who will hear all these statutes and say, 'Surely this great nation is a wise and understanding people.'*
>
> *"For what great nation is there that has a god so near to it as is the* LORD *our God whenever we call on Him?*

*"Or what great nation is there that has
statutes and judgments as righteous as this
whole law which I am setting before you
today?*

*"Only give heed to yourself and keep your
soul diligently, so that you do not forget the
things which your eyes have seen and they
do not depart from your heart all the days of
your life; but make them known to your sons
and your grandsons."*

—Deuteronomy 4:6–9

*"Now this is the commandment, the statutes
and the judgments which the LORD your God
has commanded me to teach you, that you
might do them in the land where you are
going over to possess it, so that you and your
son and your grandson might fear the LORD
your God, to keep all His statutes and His
commandments which I command you, all
the days of your life, and that your days may
be prolonged.*

*"O Israel, you should listen and be care-
ful to do it, that it may be well with you and
that you may multiply greatly, just as the
LORD, the God of your fathers, has promised
you, in a land flowing with milk and honey.*

*"Hear, O Israel! The LORD is our God, the
LORD is one!*

"You shall love the LORD your God with all your heart and with all your soul and with all your might.

"These words, which I am commanding you today, shall be on your heart.

"You shall teach them diligently to your sons and shall talk of them when you sit in your house and when you walk by the way and when you lie down and when you rise up."

—Deuteronomy 6:1–7

In Donald Whitney's book *Spiritual Disciplines for the Christian Life,* he says, "One of the main reasons for a lack of Godliness is prayerlessness."

I would say that prayer was the cornerstone in our home in my growing-up years. My brothers, sisters, and I have a great family heritage in prayer. Every day as long as I can remember, my parents would pray for each of their children by name. As the family grew, they added the grandchildren, and then the great-grandchildren.

Earlier in this book I related the vivid childhood memory of hearing my father pray one fall morning. When I heard him pray that day, I could tell he and God were friends. However, when my father completed his book, *Prayer of the Heart,* in 2005, he told me that it was my mother who taught him to pray. What a tribute to his life partner of 62 years! Yes, my mother was a woman of prayer and a woman of the Word. My mother related everything to Scripture. She was not a highly educated woman, but she was a well-read woman, and she loved the Word of God. I often say we were raised over our dad's knees—and at our mother's knees.

One day in a visit with my mother before she passed away, she asked me this question, "Esther, do you ever speak to wives of ministers?"

"Yes, sometimes," was my reply.

"Well, I shared with a group of young women recently that every Sabbath morning, I would lay out your father's clothes on the bed for him—his suit, tie, hanky, socks, and shoes." She said that she was surprised when they laughed at her; she had not intended to be humorous. Their response was, "Let them dress themselves!"

"I remember you did that for Dad. Why did you do it?" I thought it might be a rule in some minister's wife handbook!

She replied quietly with these piercing words: "I did it so that your father could have more time on his knees before God, as he prepared to go to the pulpit and open the Word of God for the people of God."

I came away from that conversation feeling deeply convicted. I did not serve my husband in that manner. So—you guessed it—the very next Sunday, I got up a bit earlier. While Bob was having a bite of breakfast with the children, I went into our bedroom and laid out a suit, shirt, tie, hankie, socks, and shoes on the bed for him. I felt so proud. He came to the bedroom to get dressed, saw his clothes on the bed, and said, "What on earth are you doing?"

"I'm laying out your clothes for you."

"Thanks, but I've been dressing myself on Sundays for all these years in our marriage, and I really don't need any assistance."

"I was just trying to help and besides, I think you are supposed to be somewhere on your knees praying!"

We laughed as I shared what my mother had told me about putting out my father's clothes. I believe this servant gift of my mother putting my father's clothing on the bed on Sabbath morning was an *act of worship* to God. I have since pondered what might happen in the homes of pastors all across the world if wives did something on Sabbath mornings to make it possible for their minister-husbands to have more time on their knees before God as they prepared to speak the Word of God to the people of God.

Being a woman of this new century, I also wonder how the family might be affected if on Monday morning, the father would get the lunches ready and help with breakfast, so the mother could be on her knees in prayer for her children as they go off to school that day and for her husband as he goes to the workplace. Let's take it a bit further. What might happen if families ate breakfast together, followed by reading God's Word and praying together? Is there any doubt that we would see a difference in our children, our husbands, and the school systems?

True Worship

As a child, I associated God with church. In fact, my early memory of God is related to the Baptist Church in Crossfield, a small town close to Calgary, Alberta, Canada. This was the church in which I met Jesus Christ as my personal Savior. A child learns early that the church is just one of the places where you go to worship God. When the time is right, parents need to help the child recognize that worship is not a place, but a personal relationship. I saw a church ad in the paper that said: *"The ultimate sanctuary is not a place...but a Person."*

One of the great truths in John 4 is the awesome news Jesus reveals about true worship. As He and the Samaritan woman dialogued about worship as He sat at the well, she learned a profound truth. She, like many of us, had her focus of worship on a *place*, not a *person*. The Samaritan woman, with the help of Jesus, made the *person* connection at the well that day. Recall that she and Jesus were having what I would call a religious conversation about where to worship and the coming Messiah. Hear Jesus's words:

> *"Woman, believe Me, an hour is coming*
> *when neither in this mountain nor in*
> *Jerusalem will you worship the Father. You*
> *worship what you do not know; we worship*
> *what we know, for salvation is from the Jews.*
> *But an hour is coming, and now is, when*
> *the true worshipers will worship the Father in*
> *spirit and truth; for such people the Father*

> *seeks to be His worshipers. God is spirit, and*
> *those who worship Him must worship in spirit*
> *and truth."*
>
> —John 4:21–24

What profound words these were to a woman who was not allowed to worship in the inner temple, and being a Samaritan woman, was shunned by the Messiah's own people. These were indeed profound words! Look what happens next. The woman had enough religious information to say, *"I know that Messiah is coming"* and *"when that One comes, He will declare all things to us"* (John 4:25). Jesus, the Messiah, said to her, *"I who speak to you am He"* (John 4:26). A literal translation reads: The One who speaks to you is I AM. She and the Messiah— communing together! Jesus chose to reveal Himself to a woman...a Samaritan woman. ***Amazing grace!***

The Samaritan woman was challenged by Jesus to consider who He was. Because of this encounter, she was to become the first evangelist missionary. The moment she recognized the truth of who He was, she ran to share the good news. She had met the Messiah. What an altar of worship that experience was for her! Just as the Samaritan woman met Jesus by the well, you and I can choose to meet Jesus daily and lead our children to meet Him through family altar in our homes, helping our children learn to personally seek daily encounters with Him.

Let's reflect for a moment on the ultimate altar. Jesus's death on the cross was the ultimate sacrifice—the *ultimate altar,* which, when we come to Jesus there, brings us directly into a personal relationship with Him.

The Purpose of Family Altar

My husband and I chose to celebrate the tradition of family altar differently from the way either of our families of origin practiced it. We firmly believe God's instruction in Deuteronomy 6. It is the responsibility of the parents to give religious instruction to the children. The church can and will assist...but the primary work is for the parents! This is very difficult in today's culture; in so many families, both parents work. Richard Foster, the wonderfully thoughtful and gifted Quaker writer, says these dramatic words: "The closest thing to a family altar in America is the TV! We worship it."

Family altar builds *traditions*—which bring *solidarity* to the home. The earlier the family can begin the tradition of family altar, the easier it will be to maintain, even during the teen years. The experts tell us today that the father can impact his children while they are still in the mother's womb...by talking to them...and playing music for them. Why not start family altar that early?

Many years ago, I was visiting in the home of a young couple stationed in Germany. Their little baby was just six weeks old. Every evening when the child was put to bed, the young father stood at his crib and read the Bible to him. You might wonder: *What impact could that possibly have?* First, from birth, the father took time with the baby, and the baby loved his daddy's voice. Second, the Word of God is the *Word of God*. It is full of truth and life. What better reading could there be?

Establishing family altar as a tradition in your home takes intentional, focused commitment to obey God's commands. Most often these days, the workload for this commitment falls to the mother.

In biblical times, Jewish boys by the age of 13 started wearing phylacteries, called *tefillin,* during weekday morning prayers. Phylacteries were two black leather cubes with long leather straps. The cubes encased passages from the Torah written on strips of parchment. At the beginning of the day, these prayers were said. You might think that a strange tradition, but it was this very tradition that taught these young men the Scriptures.

We already know that children learn from repetition. Therefore, if we teach our children God's Word in family altar, we are fulfilling two of our duties stated in Deuteronomy 6:4–9: keeping God's Word on our hearts and instilling it and its truth into their hearts and eventually into their lives.

Because family altar was a tradition in our home, we observed it whether everyone wanted to observe it or not. Our children did not have a choice in this matter. It is one of those items parents control by virtue of being the parent, and it wields power just in the fact that a tradition does not have to be explained—just done.

We used the calendar year to help make preparation for worship for family altar in our home. For example, we have always had a worship service following our Thanksgiving meal. It has always been a very special time…and a time to which we would look forward because of the creativity and planning that always goes into this service. Everyone who joined our family circle around that Thanksgiving table was involved in this service with us because we always have a response time. As our children grew older, they were given responsibility in helping with the planning and producing of our worship time—under the leadership of their dad.

When our daughter, Melody, came home for Thanksgiving during her first semester in college, my parents, my baby sister, and her husband were celebrating with us. I will never forget that day! I had asked Bob to go a bit easy on the thankful response time…knowing the circumstances of family members present on this special day. He was very sensitive in his leadoff statement; it went something like this:

"I know everyone here has much for which to be thankful this year, so why don't I just voice a prayer of thanks for all of us."

We were all startled at what happened next!

"Wait, just a minute!" said Melody. "I have something to say. I wish no one was here except Mom, Dad, and Big Dave, 'cause what I want to say is none of anyone's darn (or something similar) business but mine."

Eyes open wide, I took a big breath, glanced over at my mother, wondering what on earth she was thinking about this outburst in our worship time. My heart was quickly quieted with my daughter's next words.

"This time last year and probably the year before, I hated this family altar stuff. But now that I'm in college and I've experienced a lot of things and been with kids whose homes are not at all like mine, I want to say thank you for always having family altar—'cause it's made our home different, and I have come to appreciate it. [Long pause.] I'm done, Dad. Now you can pray."

That was prayer enough for me. Traditions don't have to be explained. It's tradition...and you do it...building solidarity in the home...centered at the altar of worship. Parents, be faithful in your altar time in your homes.

The Focus of Family Altar

> *Joshua said, "By this you shall know that the living God is among you."*
>
> —Joshua 3:10

Recall with me the event in Scripture when Joshua was instructed to bring the ark of the covenant across the Jordan (Joshua 3–4). *"And the priests who carried the ark of the covenant of the LORD stood firm on dry ground in the middle of the Jordan while all Israel crossed on dry ground, until all the nation had finished crossing the Jordan"* (Joshua 3:17).

Then God instructed Joshua to take 12 men—one from each tribe—and tell each to take a stone from the middle of the Jordan and place the stones by the place where they would lodge that night. Joshua then stated the purpose of this activity: *"Let this be a sign among you, so that when your children ask later, saying, 'What do these stones mean to you?'* then you shall say to them, 'Because the waters of the Jordan were cut off before the ark of the covenant of the LORD; when it crossed the Jordan, the waters of the Jordan were cut off.' So these stones shall become a memorial to the sons of Israel forever" (Joshua 4:6–7).

Earlier, when the sons of Israel were camped by the Jordan, the officers had gone through the camp telling the people that when they see the ark of the covenant coming through their camp, they should follow it. Then Joshua said to Israel, *"Consecrate yourselves, for tomorrow the LORD will do wonders among you"* (Joshua 3:5).

God spoke to Joshua, telling him: *"This day I will begin to exalt you in the sight of all Israel, that they may know that just as I have been with Moses, I will be with you"* (Joshua 3:7).

Imagine Joshua's joy when he said to God's people: *"Come here, and hear the words of the LORD your God...By this you shall know that the living God is among you* [and is working out His plan for you]*"* (Joshua 3:9–10). What a great word for families today. Family altar helps families experience God working in their homes. Those of us who practice family altar too can truly say the living God is among us and working His plan for our future!

A Psalm 37 Solution

A wonderful book entitled *The Grandmother Book* (now out of print), written by grandmothers Jan Stoop and

Betty Southard taught me to pray Psalm 37:3–7 for the children.

> *Trust in the L*ORD *and do good;*
> *Dwell in the land and cultivate faithfulness.*
> *Delight yourself in the L*ORD*;*
> *And He will give you the desires of your*
>   *heart.*
> *Commit your way to the L*ORD*,*
> *Trust also in Him, and He will do it.*
> *He will bring forth your righteousness as*
>   *the light*
> *And your judgment as the noonday.*
> *Rest in the L*ORD *and wait patiently for Him;*
> *Do not fret because of him who prospers in*
>   *his way,*
> *Because of the man who carries out wicked*
> *schemes.*
>
> —Psalm 37:3–7

In this book, Betty Southard said: "I take my problem, whatever it is, and I figuratively lay it out on my hands, palms facing upward. I specifically state what it is, and then I turn my hands down, palms open, and let the problem drop into God's hands. When I commit the problem to Him, I have relinquished my problem to the Lord."

All of us probably have trouble with that. The psalmist says to *"commit our ways"* (troubles) to the Lord, and then he tells us to trust Him to take care of them. Betty goes on to say: "It is immediately at this point that I find Satan whispering his little lies in my ear: 'That's too minor to bother the Lord with. Why don't you just handle this one yourself?' 'Who do you think you are that you can ask God to do that for you?' 'So you really think He cares about that?' 'What if the Lord doesn't work it out the way you want?' The doubts and fears crop up immediately."

So what does Betty do? "By an act of faith, not feelings, I simply reply, 'Thank You, Lord, for I know You are taking care of my problem. Lord, I believe. Help my unbelief.'"

After turning the problem over to the Lord, the next steps are delighting in the Lord, praising Him, and thanking Him for what He can and will do. To help remember the steps of this prayer of thanks, those two grandmothers say you can use this acrostic made with the letters of the word *delight:*

> **D** aily
> **E** verything
> **L** aid
> **I** nto
> **G** od's
> **H** ands
> **T** otally

These authors tell us to repeat this phrase over and over to remind ourselves that we have committed our problem to the Lord. Then we are able to move on and rest in the Lord, because in addition to committing to the Lord and trusting and delighting in Him, the psalmist tells us to *"rest in the LORD"* (Psalm 37:7).

Recently, I have literally held my hands up to Him in adoration. I have been praying this prayer over my adult children for several months now, as well as for my grandchildren—and the line that I cry out to God so often is this: *"I believe. Help my unbelief"* (see Mark 9:23). Then I have emptied my heart into His hands with specific requests.

My prayer journal shows His faithfulness as I have marked off the requests with words of gratitude. I have delighted in rejoicing with my daughter's family as a contract on their home was signed in just two days...and a home was bought in one day...at the right price...near a good school. I had joined her family in praying as I specifically laid in God's hands the price, the place, a church, and a peace for her about the right home—that as she walked into the house, she would know it was the right home for them. How wonderful to see the God of Israel at work in this place (home). I don't know how her family celebrated this event, but "Nana and Bop" (our grandmother and grandfather names) made an altar of tears before the Father— thanking God that He, the living God, is at work among us! And that He is still at work so *specifically* in our lives.

Nana's Summer Camp

When visiting in our home one time, the Trinkles, fellow church members, told us about a family tradition they practice yearly: Gramma's Summer Camp. I was impressed and inspired as I listened to them describe it. Mothers and children gathered each summer for one week at the grandparents' home. I was so touched when I heard about aunts teaching nieces and nephews and by cousins bonding into lifetime friends that I just knew we had to make it happen for the Burroughs clan.

In the summer of 1998, we held the first ever Nana's Summer Camp. Our three grandgirls, Anna, Caroline, and Frances—at that time, ages 9, 7, and 5—and their parents came to our home in Jacksonville, Florida, for four and one-half days. The Nana's Summer Camp theme signs posted on the garage door welcomed all campers with these words: "I am a promise. I am a possibility!"

Upon entering the front door, and after hugs and kisses, the campers were taken to the kitchen where room assignments and all camps rules were posted on the kitchen cabinet doors. Camp had begun!

We learned the theme song, "I Am a Promise, I Am a Possibility." We learned, "I can be anything...anything God wants me to be."

We read the story of Noah and the ark in preparation for a closing drama presentation we would prepare during the camp—using Noah's ark and Beanie Babies. Each morning and afternoon, we were involved in interesting activities, such as designing our own camp T-shirts, going to a water park, visiting a pottery works and making our own pottery items, preparing a drama production, swimming, memorizing Scripture, and fishing. We had some down time, too, for resting and watching movies.

My favorite time was the birthday breakfast for all three girls. Since Bob and I are seldom with them on their real birthdays, we decided to do it all at one time. Anna helped Bop fix his famous family breakfast. Caroline set the table, and Frances helped by putting the silverware on the table. After the meal and before we gave their gifts, each person was given a sheet of paper on which was drawn a gift box, wrapped in a bow with a tag that read *"You are special."* Anna printed the name of each family member on the left side of the gift box. I instructed the family to give a *word gift* to each family member by writing a special word beside each person's name. When everyone had finished, we went around the table and each person told out loud the *word gift* they had written for each of the other persons. It was a holy moment!

Creative Anna added Twin #1 and Twin #2 at the bottom of the page, because our son and his wife were expecting twins in September of 1998, and we were all excited about it. Sensitive Caroline, the middle daughter, wrote the word *hopeful* by both Twin #1 and Twin #2. I cried. Then Bop prayed a blessing, naming quality traits of each person at the table, and a special blessing on the expected twins and their parents. This birthday breakfast became an *altar of thanksgiving*—focusing our family on gratitude.

The Place and Time for Family Altar

Building an altar before God in the home unites and strengthens the family in a way that nothing else can do. One denomination for years used the slogan, "The family that prays together stays together." Whether worshiping together in church as they sit together as a family or worshiping together in the home, families make a statement about themselves when they choose to worship God as a family.

The place of family altar can be rather simple: wherever the family meets frequently. The place can and should vary, but *the habit must not vary*, for it needs to be consistent. Family altar simply means the family takes time to celebrate their commitment to God by planning time to pray and read God's Word together... *consistently*. Possibilities abound for where and when to have family altar.

Living room or bedroom at bedtime. Fluffy pillows and down comforters make for soft cuddling and help create an opportune environment for nightly prayers and the reading of the Bible and other good books. As tiny babies, my granddaughters were rocked and sung to sleep by their father until they were big enough to sing with him "Jesus Loves Me" and "Hush Little Baby." Nighttime prayers, along with Bible stories or chapter books, give way to words of love and comfort as children prepare for sleep. I know one family who allows each child to choose two books each evening, and one of the two must be a Bible story. This is great reinforcement to what they get in Sunday school. So many of the Bible stories teach moral truths by which to live; reading and rereading them instills truth into their hearts. When reading a story for the umpteenth time, remember, don't skip any words...or the children will let you know it!

Around the table. Families of my generation gathered around tables at home, at our grandparents' homes, at friends' homes. More than food was shared: life stories were told and retold; God's stories were told; laughter and tears were mixed together. If you grew up in a home with a kitchen table, you know that's where everything is dumped: backpacks after school, sports bags, groceries from the market, books from the library, Bibles and Sunday school lesson books, heartaches, relationship problems—everything. How about turning that table into an altar? Oh, I know it doesn't look like an altar most of the time, but if life is shared around the table that is covered with love, concern, kindness, prayer, and Bible verses, that turns a dumped-on table into an altar. Everyday moments offer opportunities for the kitchen table to become an altar: A mother leans over a child coloring, and says, "O darling, what an artist you are! I thank God for your gift with colors." A wife, leaning down to gently hug her husband as he writes checks to pay bills, whispers, "I really thank God for your gifts and strengths that provide for our family." An older sister affirms a little sister as she does her homework. A friend listens over coffee to your heartbreak and prays for you.

When people are gathered around a table and use the Lord's name in expressing a blessing or thanksgiving, a table becomes an altar.

Seemingly, the art of eating together is a family tradition that is about to be lost! Family experts tell us that the only night the entire American family is together these days is Sunday night! This can be a great time for family night and family worship. It can be like getting a head start in preparing the family to begin another week. Perhaps the family can miss Sunday evening church every so often to get things ready in advance and not feel so rushed. This, of course, is not an option for most church staff families.

Family nights. My daughter's family has a special family night dinner with special dishes and candles. They use this time to discuss responsibilities related to their chores, their allowances, and such. This is a perfect time to share prayer requests for each other and close with sentence prayers.

When our children were growing up, we had family night on Friday nights. Family members took turns choosing the activity for that evening (bowling was my least favorite), planning and helping prepare the meal for the event, setting and clearing the table, or occasionally selecting a restaurant. Everyone shared in the conversation around the table. For a period of time, the family member who told the funniest story from their week received the dollar that was placed on the refrigerator with a magnet. This little tactic helped ensure table conversation. We found this meal was an excellent time to discuss issues that affected our family, school, and community. On these evenings, we planned worship after the evening's event. Most family events are opportunities for altar times, building family unity in Christ, and building family memories.

December mealtimes. I am acquainted with families that celebrate family altar each mealtime in the month of December. As Christmas cards arrive, one card is selected from the card basket and the note and name of the sender are read. The blessing always includes the family or friend who sent the card. What a wonderful way to be a blessing to others. This December altar can be extended as long as there are cards representing families for whom to pray.

Among families. One year as our family set our goals for the upcoming year, we asked two other families with the same configuration as ours if they would like to enter into a prayer covenant with us for one year. Members of both families said yes. The parents prayed for the other mothers and fathers, and the children prayed for each other. These three families all lived in different cities, so calls and letters furnished prayer requests and answers. If I were doing this today, I would stay in contact with aunts/uncles/cousins or other covenant family by email, which is another great way to keep families connected. Email becomes an *ongoing altar*, you might say.

Whole home. Bob and I have always dedicated each of our homes to the Lord. You see, our home does not belong to us…it might legally belong to a bank, but ultimately it is the Lord's! We are to be stewards of the home and use it in such a way that it is a blessing to the Father.

When we moved to West Palm Beach, where Bob was to teach at Palm Beach Atlantic College, we bought an old home near the Intercoastal Waterway. We pulled up the carpet and found someone to sand the beautiful hardwood floors. What a delight to discover, as we went in and out to check on the progress, that blessings were being voiced in our new-to-us home. I was unpacking boxes in the room that was to be my office as Jerry, the craftsman working on our floors, was putting the finishing touches on the dining room floor and singing. He stopped singing and began to pray. I stopped to listen.

"Father, I consecrate this dining room floor to You. I've done my best and I've used my gifts, but now I consecrate these floors to You and pray that everybody that comes in Bob and Esther's home and sits around their table will feel Your love." Then he prayed over the living room and the bedroom and continued to consecrate and pray over every room in the house. I was standing in my office with tears running down my face, saying to the Lord, "We always dedicate our home to You but I've never had anyone consecrate our home even before we moved in." Jerry stopped praying and moved out of the kitchen and through the garage. I knew he was coming to the front door, and I did not know whether to tell him I'd secretly joined him in his worship service, but it was so obvious as the tears ran down my face. I said, "Oh, Jerry! Bob and I thank you for consecrating our home to the Lord." Our home—an altar of thanksgiving!

Any room in your home can be an altar before the Lord. If it is true that we have lost our influence in the home, perhaps we can start afresh and make the kitchen or dining table the center of family gatherings where the Word, joys, laughter, tears, conversations, and struggles are all shared, prayed over with grace, and given to the Father for His ever-watchful care.

I remember a time when our children were in grade school and our TV was broken. It was several weeks before the TV was returned to our family room. Upon its return, our son, David, said, "I wish the TV was still broken—'cause we talked to each other more often and played games together." That was amazing insight from a child who watched limited TV, but it was a profound truth. It is easy to go through life letting the blaring TV consume valuable family time. Without the noise and distraction of the TV, we talk to each other more. Make opportunities for altar times in the family room—and try turning off the TV.

Seasonal celebrations. Use the seasons as times of celebration for the gift and opportunities of that season. Check out some library books related to Thanksgiving, Christmas, and Easter. Look for creative ways to involve the family in planning worship celebrations. With the children, make a Christmas calendar marking the number of days until December 25; it can be a banner calendar with a pocket for each day or a Christmas tree–shaped calendar. This could be very elaborate or simple, with homemade Christmas items or simple crayon-colored items to place in each pocket on the banner or on the tree to help the children count down the days from December 1 to Christmas day.

Plan a family evening in November to make the banner and items to be placed in every pocket. The mom will have to gather the material prior to the planned evening. Let all family members have a part in the preparation. Make a big event of hanging the banner! Tell the children they will take turns each day until the 25th...daily taking an item from the pocket and placing it on the tree. After completing the project, build a fire in the fireplace, gather the children around the fireplace, pop popcorn, snuggle under a favorite quilt or blanket, and have the dad read part of the Christmas story. Have the mother pray a blessing for each child by name, thanking God that they can celebrate Jesus's birthday together. An altar time indeed!

Video night. Depending on the ages of the children, have a video night, choosing videos that teach family values. After viewing the video, have a family dialogue about the truth taught. Relate this to a recent family situation, if possible. Open the Word of God to teach your children reliance on God's promises and principles. Close the evening with prayer time—always giving the children an opportunity to pray. Family worship—in the family room!

Family retreat. Retreat events are very popular today. When our children were in grade school, my parents were coming to visit for the Christmas holidays. I thought, *Why not plan a family retreat that would take place in the family room on special evenings after dinner?* With my parents living a great distance away—Canada, California, and Texas at different times— and both families being in ministry, our children had not been around my parents very much. My purpose was to help my children and their grandparents get better acquainted with each other and perhaps discover a new way to look at Christmas.

We began the week by Christmas caroling for all the neighbors on Monday. We were new to the neighborhood that year and wanted to get to know our neighbors, so earlier in the day Monday, the children and I prepared goody baskets for all the neighbors. (Yes, the kitchen was a mess, but when you get your family involved in activities such as this, you are teaching values and virtues that last a lifetime, so forget the mess!) Then caroling we went—children, parents, and grandparents—singing on the doorsteps of our neighbors' homes. As we began singing at each home, the lights would come on quickly and the family would appear at the door. Each family seemed delighted as we sang Christmas carols. After singing, we wished them a Merry Christmas, presented our gift of goodies, and walked away. Tabitha, our family kitten, even went with us, tagging along right behind. Caroling gave us a chance to meet our neighbors and to leave the fragrance of Christ as we sang the message of Christ's birth. We were asked the next year if we would carol again.

Tuesday night, I assigned parts of the Christmas story to the children and grandparents. They were instructed to go to separate rooms, read the Scripture on the card I had given them, and prepare a skit to present to the whole family. David, age 10, was to pretend to be the innkeeper's son and his grandfather, the innkeeper. Pretending the son had been standing just outside the stable and had seen the baby and his mother, David was to tell the story through the eyes of that innkeeper's son. Melody, age 13, and her grandmother were to tell the story of Mary explaining to her mother that she was to have a baby that would be named Jesus. Bob and I told the story of the shepherds' experience through the eyes of the shepherds. I wish I could have put this worship time on tape, but in those days, VCRs were not around yet! I certainly treasure the memory of that sweet time together.

Wednesday night, we shared family traditions from both my parents' growing-up homes. My parents and I grew up in Canada, so that added interest for my children. In winter, my dad would take the hose and water down the garden until it froze to make a skating rink. Our children loved hearing their parents' and grandparents' stories of celebrating Christmas in the "olden days." Children enjoy stories, especially about people they love. If you ever tell your children stories of your growing up days, they will beg you to tell the good ones over and over. Think of this as passing on your heritage.

Thursday night, we prepared a basket and gifts for a needy family in our city, teaching our children to share what we have been given. My daughter now has three girls of her own, and this is one of their Christmas family traditions. They bake, shop, and wrap gifts together, sharing Christ's love with other families.

My memory is that our Christmas family retreat was very meaningful to our small family. We didn't have to leave town for our family retreat. It took place mostly in our family room and kitchen. Still, it required considerable work and preparation...but we got a lot of help from the children. The more we let the children help with family altar, the more meaningful it becomes to them. Remember, an altar helps the family *focus* and worship no matter what place or time you choose to celebrate.

The Plan for Family Altar

To have a successful family altar, it must be put on the family calendar along with other important dates. Having a successful family altar takes planning. Someone has to do the behind-the-scenes stuff. If you have never done this before and are just now thinking about beginning, call the family together and share with them what you want to do—that you want to be obedient to God in leading your family in scriptural truth. You may need to apologize for not having done this in the past, but you and your family need to choose to begin it today. Little children will accept it. Teens may not like it, but they will most likely feel safe and loved in the fact that you care enough to begin an altar time.

Any time is a good time to start, but start slowly. Most families cannot do family altar today the way my parents did years ago for the obvious reason that today's family schedules are more hectic and families seldom eat together around the table. If you start off trying to do it every day, you may find that difficult to accomplish. However, if you carefully plan for a family worship time twice a month, you will probably succeed in accomplishing that goal. Family altar does not have to mean by definition that all family members must be present every time. A mother and son could enjoy an afternoon of shopping and a quiet dinner together. A father and daughter could plan to have some time together with the intention of sharing meaningful life conversations and promising to pray about ideas discussed, or even pray together at her bedside later that night.

When our daughter was to get married, I planned way ahead to have time with her by myself on the day of the rehearsal dinner. We got home in the afternoon and piled onto her bed. I read one of her favorite bedtime stories to her, *The Velveteen Rabbit*. Then we talked about the facts that she was starting her own home and, at the same time, would be getting a whole new family on her husband's side. We discussed what all that would come to mean. We cried, and we laughed. I pointed out the bottom line, "You must continue to become real with yourself and family," and how "that would be a good rule to live by—one that would please the Father." Then we prayed together.

When our son got married, Bob and I wanted to give him a significant gift of love and came up with the idea to write our long-time friends (many of whom had grown with us in the ministry) and ask them to provide words of wisdom and counsel about marriage to our son as he began his married life. Many of these special friends had watched David grow and mature to manhood and had prayed with us through the years as we raised our family. It was such a treasure to be able to give our son and his bride, Colleen, these words of wisdom from our brothers and sisters in Christ.

Family altar...

...is looking for opportunities to see eternal significance in everyday matters.

...is seeing the sacred in the ordinary and catching the moment.

...creates lasting memories.

Begin by setting goals, and have an action plan to carry out the goals.

- Check the family calendar; find a spot and mark it "Family!"
- Go to the bookstore and purchase age-appropriate family worship idea books.

- Gather needed material.
- Jot down an order of events:
    Bible story
    Bible truth and memory verse
    Questions
    Prayer time
- Look ahead for worship opportunities, such as dedication of your home, Thanksgiving worship, special dinner with close friends, Christmas events, or outdoor worship.

These special worship times will take careful planning and preparation ahead of time, so you won't be overwhelmed at the last minute.

Plan around events, such as after church on Sunday night. If you don't have Sunday night church, that is a wonderful time to begin family altar. Plan a family dinner, using your best china for your best guests—your family. Share with the children the responsibilities in preparation of the meal and in planning family worship time.

As our children grew older, they were given the opportunity to plan the altar time and to lead the family in worship. This is a wonderful way to encourage their gifts and abilities. Special events at church offer more opportunities to invite friends over for dessert. End the time by singing around the piano and offering prayers and blessings for the next week.

When we moved to Jacksonville, Florida, for Bob to become the director of church music for the Florida

Baptist Convention, our children were grown and in homes of their own, so we purposefully chose a smaller home; therefore, we did not need all our furniture. We offered the extra furniture to our children. They took us up on the offer. David and his dad loaded the rental truck, which David would be driving back to Louisville, Kentucky, making a stop at his sister's on the way. As David and Colleen prepared to leave, we asked them if we could pray over the furniture, because it had been a blessing to us, had graced our home, and had been shared with many guests, and we wanted to pass that blessing along. In the driveway with David and Colleen, we shared a Scripture and prayed over the furniture and the truck—asking God to bless the furniture in their home, to give them joy in its use, and to give them safe travel. A driveway can become an altar.

Before any trip we took during my childhood, my father prayed and asked for *journeying mercies*. Different people make the same type request in different ways. One lady, who picked me up at an airport to take me to a speaking engagement, prayed as we got into the car, "Put an angel on every wheel, God...we're out of here!" And off we went—both laughing in God's presence!

The Presence at the Altar

Family altar offers opportunity for the family to experience the *presence of God* in the home.

Not every altar time will be holy or even memorable. Only once did Jesus take three of His disciples to the mount where they saw Moses and Elijah. Peter was so overwhelmed that he wanted to stay. Then Peter, James, and John were so surprised by God's voice from heaven affirming His Son that they fell on their faces. What a holy interruption! Again, this happened only *one* time. Most of the time the disciples were with Jesus, He was providing long teaching sessions on hillsides, walking dusty roads, storytelling, and cooking fish at campfires. There are probably times you walked out of worship on Sunday morning and whispered quietly to your mate: "The Spirit was present this morning." But you don't say it every Sunday, do you? All God asks is for worship with the proper attitude and adoration. The issue here is not about the altar being *holy*, but about the heart being *humble* and obedient to God's commands.

Ever since our son, David, was in the first grade, we have celebrated Advent in our home. The meaning of Advent is simply, *coming*. Advent seemed such a natural event for family worship. I bought a book that showed us how to make an Advent wreath and how to select the Scriptures for the four weeks of celebration.

We desired to teach our children the spiritual significance of Advent. The repetition of the ritual each year programmed into their hearts the promises of God. We looked up the Old Testament prophecy...then looked for the fulfillment in the New Testament...and memorized a Scripture verse about Christ's promised return. It took time the first year to write out all the memory verses—placing the verses on star symbols with a string attached for placement on the wreath.

When we first started our Advent celebration, the children were only old enough to argue about who lit the candles every night. But they were getting the ritual of it, and I knew they would get the meaning of the laws and precepts of God as the years went by. When we first began celebrating Advent, we made the wreath and took time to worship every night. As the children grew, we did Advent on Sundays only.

One year, we chose to worship as a family from Advent all the way through to Easter. After Christmas, David took our Christmas tree, cut off all the branches, and made a cross from the limbs of the tree. He hammered the cross into a block of wood, allowing it to stand. Yes, it looked like a child made it. The nails were sticking up all over the bottom. We used that cross for 18 years in our home on special worship occasions. It became the center of worship for us, and it drew us together.

It was our children who taught us in the Lenten season that year to give up some meals so we could give the money to those who were hungry.

I'll never forget the special times we had during Scripture reading with the children that Holy Week before Easter: It was as if the starlight of the cradle was being extinguished, as life got darker and darker for Jesus and His disciples that last week. We had put candles around the foot of the cross, and each day in worship, we extinguished a candle. We talked on Good Friday about what the disciples must have felt in losing their friend. When we got to Saturday's worship time, we listened to a cassette of Keith Miller tell the story of the crucifixion in the first person as if he were Matthew. We could hear those nails being pounded into the cross, and little David, who was not a Christian at the time, cried out: "Momma! No! Don't let them kill Jesus!" I said, "Oh, David. He had to die. That's why He came. But David, Easter Sunday morning, we will celebrate His resurrection from the grave!" The Christian faith is the only faith that celebrates the risen, living Christ. Alleluia! What a Savior!

After listening to the tape, I covered the cross with a black cloth shroud. We talked about losing our puppy and how that death felt to us as a family. (That was the only death we'd experienced in our family at the time.) We were trying to teach how Jesus's friends must have felt in losing Him and their wrong thinking that He was going to set up an earthly kingdom.

Early on Easter Sunday morning, I got up and lifted the shroud from the cross, replaced the candles with fresh daisies, and put the black cloth shroud back over the cross. I put on a record—the music from *Celebrate Life*, "He is alive! He is alive! He is alive!" I ran upstairs into Melody's room, opened her door, and shouted: "Get up! Get up! It's Easter Sunday morning! He is alive!" We then went to David's room saying the same thing: "Get up! Get up! It's Easter Sunday morning! He is alive!" We got to Papa's room last, and we burst in with these same words: "Get up! Get up! It's Easter Sunday morning!

He is alive!" We all ran down to the den, and David lifted off that shroud and saw the daisies. He was wide-eyed with surprise, and the four of us sat on the floor of that Birmingham home singing together through our tears, "He is alive! He is alive! He is alive!" You know what? We really didn't need to go to big church that Sunday! We already had had *big* church. But, oh no, my friends! When you make an altar in your home, then it draws you back to the body of Christ to worship before our Holy God! *Surely, the presence of the Lord is in this place.* The *presence* at the altar was real for the Burroughs family that Easter Sunday!

Splashed and Splashing

1. Read John 4:20–24. What does Jesus tell us about true worship?
2. Write the key word that is found in all three of these Scriptures:

   Genesis 22:5

   Deuteronomy 6:13

   2 Chronicles 29:28
3. Whether married or single, do you have family altar in your home?
4. Describe your own quiet time of worship.
5. If you desire to begin family altar, list your goals.

More Splashing

Visit a local Christian bookstore, and browse through the Family or Worship book sections. Carefully select age-appropriate books to help you build a family altar.

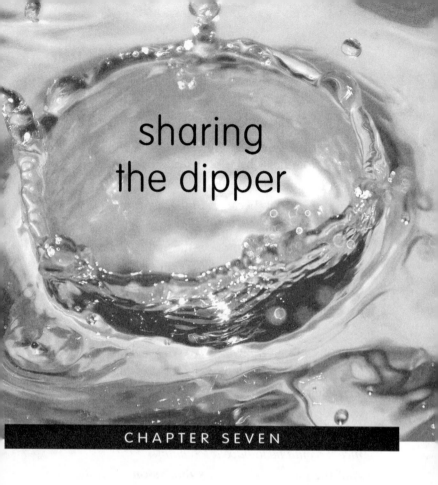

sharing
the dipper

Throughout His ministry, Jesus asked people for certain things He needed—while at the same time, engaging them in conversation, which often led to His being able to minister to them. On one occasion, He asked a man for a pitcher of water and a room where He then proceeded to serve His disciples the last supper. We cannot forget that He asked His disciples to ask a man for the use of his donkey for His triumphant entry into Jerusalem as the Suffering Servant King!

Such was the case that hot afternoon at the well in Samaria, when He asked the woman for a drink. Because He asked her to serve Him the water, He then had the opportunity to offer her life-giving water. Many people from her village came to know Him as personal Savior because He and the woman had shared a dipper of water and it became **living water** to her. What a splash that made!

On another occasion near the end of His earthly ministry, Jesus had just shared in a last meal with His disciples when He dealt with the fact that the basic necessity of hospitality for that day had not been provided: He washed their feet. After the experience of speaking in Cairo, Egypt, I have a whole new appreciation for the hospitable practice of washing your guest's feet—dusty and dirty from road travel. Everywhere we walked, the dust made itself at home on our feet and clothes. Several times during my stay, I thought, *How nice it would be to have a footbath!*

If the cross is a sign of **submission**, then the towel must then be the sign of **servanthood.** When Jesus washed His disciples' feet, He set the servanthood example for us to follow. He picked up a towel, poured water in a basin, and modeled a lifestyle for you and me.

> *"Just as the Son of Man did not come to be served, but to serve, and to give His life a ransom for many."*
>
> —Matthew 20:28

Richard Foster in his book *Celebration of Discipline* invites his readers to "live simply, so others may simply live." What a challenge to the Christian culture!

> Our culture says **get for yourself.**
> Jesus says **give of yourself.**
>
> Our culture says **be yourself.**
> Jesus says **deny yourself.**
>
> Our culture says **find yourself.**
> Jesus says **lose yourself.**

I recently heard a bank advertisement announcing a loan program. The announcer said these astounding words: "It makes sense to have it, even if you don't need it." I thought to myself, *only in America would one believe such a lie.* We might ask ourselves the question, *When is enough enough?* We must choose to live as Great Commission Christians—making a difference in our world for the sake of Christ. My challenge for you in this chapter is to live intentionally—*sharing the dipper.*

If You Have Some, Give Some

Some years ago, I was invited to write an article on the subject of servanthood. In my preparation to write, I called a missionary friend in South Florida for an interview. After our opening greetings, I said, "John, tell me what you do in South Florida that I can share with teenagers that will inspire them to touch their world with Christ's love?" He quietly laughed, thought a moment, and then told me the following story.

When he and Barbara, his wife, arrived in South Florida, it was evident that they needed to begin some kind of ministry to the migrant farm workers and their families. The children needed food and proper clothing as well as help with school lessons. He called a group of pastors together in the neighborhood, presented the needs of these underresourced migrants, and asked for their help. Many were eager to help. They went back to their congregations and presented the plan.

They asked for teachers to volunteer after school and in the evenings to tutor these children. They asked for families in their churches to gather food and clothing to share with the migrant children. They requested toys and school supplies. They also asked for volunteers to do children's programs on Saturday mornings. It all seemed overwhelming—until it was given to the women's missions group—who organized it beautifully and carried out the plans. We can always count on women to have a heart for those in need.

Some months later, a building was secured and stocked with all necessary supplies, and enough volunteers were ready to assist.

I thought to myself as John gave me the details, *this sounds a lot like the early church!*

Word spread quickly about services offered at the mission center. Shortly after the center opened, an old car drove up in the front of the mission center and a young woman got out of the car and came into the center, with two small children following. (I sensed John smiling over the phone as he told me about it.) The little fella had diapers hanging down to the ground—in need of a diaper change—and the little girl's hair looked like it needed a good brushing. He thought to himself, *I wonder what kind of momma this lady is?*...when he heard God whisper, "Remember the little ones."

"Can I help you?" he asked.

"Is this the place you get them clothes?"

"Yes, it is."

"What do ya got to do to git some?"

"Just help yourself, lady, but...we do have a rule here."

"What kinda rule?"

"Our rule is this: *If you have some, give some. If you need some, take some.*"

The lady helped herself to many items of clothing and food. John cared for the children as she loaded up the supplies. Walking her to the car, he helped her fill out an information card, which would enable the mission center to follow up with the family needs.

Although feeling good about his first customer, John was certainly not prepared for a return visit from that customer two weeks later! The same car pulled up in front of the mission center, and the same lady got out of the old car with two bags in her hands—but no children by her side. She came in the front door, and without even saying hello, she said to him, "You did say the rule was *if you have some, give some,* didn't you?"

"Yes," he responded, with surprise.

"Well," she said. "Here!"

Then she thrust into his hands two brown grocery sacks full of soiled baby clothes, smiled at him, and walked away.

She heard the good news! *"If you have some, give some."* She heard, and in her poverty, she gave what she had.

I will never forget those last words. Wow!

As I hung up the phone, I kept thinking of the rule about giving and taking and thought it sounded like a good definition of the body of Christ. Not only that, I was quite certain Jesus had said those very words, so I began flipping through my Bible in search of this truth. Notice how close it is to Luke 9:24: *"For whoever wishes to save his life will lose it, but whoever loses his life for My sake, he is the one who will save it."*

To Serve, Stoop

Look at the role model Jesus was for us. His challenge to the disciples—and to us—in Matthew, chapters 5, 6, and 7, is so radical! His words were so drastic in a culture so bound by rules and looking out for number one. Even His chosen disciples argued over who would be first and have the seat of honor when the Kingdom is established! The mother of the sons of Zebedee even jumped into the picture and said to Jesus, *"Command that in Your kingdom these two sons of mine may sit one on Your right and one on Your left"* (Matthew 20:21).

Jesus told that pushy mom—and the disciples—that His Father is the One who makes that choice. When the other disciples became indignant, Jesus called them to Himself for one more powerful lesson.

"You know that the rulers of the Gentiles lord it over them, and their great men exercise authority over them. It is not this way among you [What a powerful statement about being a disciple!], *but whoever wishes to become great among you shall be your servant, and whoever wishes to be first among you shall be your slave; just as the Son of Man did not come to be served, but to serve, and to give His life a ransom for many."*

—Matthew 20:25–28

These words haunt my life: *"It is not this way among you."* What might the world look like if we who call ourselves Christians lived by His words… *"It is not this way among you."* I wonder what it would be like if we learned to not always strive for first place—the highest honor, the esteem—but to be willing, like Paul, to be a doormat for Christ? I wonder….

Not only did Jesus say He came to serve, not to be served…but He lived out that truth as He interacted with His chosen disciples. Consider His teachings from the Gospel of John, chapter 13:

Jesus knew that the Father had put him in complete charge of everything, that he came from God and was on his way back to God. So he got up from the supper table, set aside his robe, and put on an apron. Then he poured water into a basin and began to wash the feet of the disciples, drying them with his apron. When he got to Simon Peter, Peter said, "Master, you wash my feet?"

Jesus answered, "You don't understand now what I'm doing, but it will be clear enough to you later."

Peter persisted, "You're not going to wash my feet—ever!"

Jesus said, "If I don't wash you, you can't be part of what I'm doing."

"Master!" said Peter. "Not only my feet, then. Wash my hands! Wash my head!"

Jesus said, "If you've had a bath in the morning, you only need your feet washed now and you're clean from head to toe. My concern, you understand, is holiness, not hygiene. So now you're clean. But not every one of you." (He knew who was betraying him. That's why he said, "Not every one of you.") After he had finished washing their feet, he took his robe, put it back on, and went back to his place at the table.

Then he said, "Do you understand what I have done to you? You address me as

'Teacher' and 'Master,' and rightly so. That is what I am. So if I, the Master and Teacher, washed your feet, you must now wash each other's feet. I've laid down a pattern for you. What I've done, you do. I'm only pointing out the obvious. A servant is not ranked above his master; an employee doesn't give orders to the employer. If you understand what I'm telling you, act like it—and live a blessed life."

—John 13:3–17 (*The Message*)

Throughout the New Testament, the Master Teacher shows us the way:

- He **stooped** to pick up little children to bless them.
- He **stooped** to write in the sand in thoughtful prelude to forgiving a sinful woman.
- He **stooped** to wipe embarrassment from Peter after his triple denial.
- He **stooped** toward Thomas to show him His nail-scarred hands.
- He **stooped** to agonize in prayer in a garden.
- He **stooped** to a cruel death on a cross—offering eternal life for all who would believe.

He lived a life of **amazing grace**—so amazing that for the most part, we still don't get it. How do I know? We still find it impossible to consistently live by the Sermon on the Mount!

To encourage you, let me share stories of others who have attempted to embrace a servant lifestyle.

A STUDENT TAUGHT ME TO STOOP

I served as the campus minister for Samford University in Birmingham, Alabama, in the 1970s. My professor-husband and I enjoyed a wonderful nine years working with those delightful students. Our lives were deeply impacted by strong student leaders all those years, and our lives are still being impacted by those individuals— even to this day—as they have now taken leadership positions throughout the United States and unto the uttermost parts of the world.

I remember well the day two particular young men hit the campus by storm. They were tall, good looking, twin brothers—Douglas and Don Sullivan. The time came for Campus Ministry elections for Doug's senior year, and he was elected president. After he took office, the members of Campus Ministries Council were sitting around the conference table one afternoon going over the last details for the upcoming retreat. Business was completed and prayer time was over when Doug asked me if he could say a word to the council. "Of course," I responded. He then asked the council to go to the office reception area and to get comfortable on the floor. He dimmed the lights and left the room.

In a matter of minutes, he walked back through the door—carrying a basin of water and having a towel draped over his shoulder. He sat down in the middle of the group—all six feet of him—with a grin on his face as wide as he was tall!

He said to us: "This year, as your president, I want to be your servant. I don't want to stand before you—but beside you. I want to serve you in such a way that you will be able to do your work on this council, serving the students on campus." Then he opened his Bible and read from John 13. "As your leader, I want to make a covenant with you to be your servant, and I would like the privilege of washing your feet." I gasped, thinking, *What a great idea! Wish I'd thought of that!* My next thought was just like that of Peter: *Not me Lord!*

Quietly, Doug began making his way around the circle of leaders, taking off their shoes and socks—amid awesome stillness—washing and drying feet. He looked into the eyes of each person and said: "I want to be your servant. Let me wash your feet." The closer he got to me, the more I pulled my legs up under my skirt—not willing to allow this student to wash my feet. Quickly, the Spirit got my attention. This was not about me—not wanting this to be done for me—it was about his willingness to do it. *Wow!*

Have you ever had your feet washed? It is both humbling and freeing. When Doug got to me, he must have sensed my shy resistance. Looking deep into my heart, he simply said: "Mrs. B, I want to serve you, too. May I wash your feet?" I nodded, as the tears poured from my heart.

You would not be surprised at all if I told you Campus Ministry had a very good year that year.

I will always be grateful for that lesson in *bending down to serve.* My life was deeply changed by that generation of students who, through their lives, challenged my ministry.

> Love that goes upward is worship.
> Love that goes outward is affection.
> Love that stoops is grace.
>
> —Donald Barnhouse

A CHURCHWOMAN TAUGHT ME TO STOOP

I was serving as mission leader of our women's mission group in the church we attended in Atlanta. Several weeks before Thanksgiving, a call came to me from the Salvation Army, asking if our women would be willing to bake turkeys to feed the homeless. I said I thought we could and would check and call them back. The Salvation Army would bring the turkeys to our church and return to pick them up after they were cooked; all we had to do was to get them roasted. I began calling the women and found wonderful willingness to do this task.

I was to speak at one of our group meetings with the older women of the church. While there, I shared the Salvation Army request. I could see most of them nodding their heads in agreement—all, that is, except Myrtle Hash, who was 70 years young. Her beautiful white head was shaking a big, emphatic *no!* Before I could think of what to say in this situation, she said, "Not me! I won't cook a turkey...but I will go to the Salvation

Army and feed the hungry on Thanksgiving." I began thinking, *I'm the leader! I think I'm supposed to think like that!* So I said, "And I'll go with you!" She said playfully, "And I'll see to that." She did; she called several times to remind me of my promise!

I made arrangements with my married daughter to eat our Thanksgiving dinner later in the day. Thanksgiving morning arrived. I went upstairs to wake our college-age son to tell him he did not have to get up, but could sleep in since we would eat later that day. (You see, he'd woken me up so often in his life that I thought it was fair to wake him.) I told him I was going to the Salvation Army to feed the homeless. As I began to walk out of his room, I heard him say, "Way to go, Mom!" As I left the room, I heard him yell, "Mom, can I go with you?"

"I'm leaving in five minutes," I said. "If you can be in the car in that time!" I knew full well he had never taken a five-minute shower in his life! But he did indeed join me—and off we went to pick up Myrtle Hash.

I must confess to you I had never done anything like this before in my life, so I thought it would be good to dress down for the assignment—only to discover when I got there, I was still dressed up!

Being a reserved person, I was most uncomfortable seeing the long lines of people spilling outside the building...waiting to be fed a Thanksgiving dinner. Young mothers with babies were in need of formula, diapers, and a hot meal—in my very own city! Older people were living in poverty, waiting for someone to show *amazing grace* to them. I found myself keeping my back to those young mothers, as I located the plastic flatware and began folding the napkins around the knives and forks. Myrtle and David went right to the kitchen to begin preparing to serve the food. Then a terrible thing happened! I ran out of plastic flatware. Just about that time, I heard my name being called out...loud enough for everyone in the shelter to hear it!

I followed the sound and saw Myrtle with her hands on her hips staring me down. "Are you serving any food?"

"Well, I was fixing the plastic ware."

"And is that what you came to do? Get in here and serve the food."

She is my elder, so I obeyed! I couldn't help but obey...she shoved a tray of food into my hands and said, *"Go!"*

I walked slowly into the eating area and quickly put the tray down on a table without making any eye contact with the person seated there. You see, I hadn't learned about *stooping* yet. I hurried back to the kitchen, and she began handing me yet another tray as she asked, "Well, what did they say?"

"I'm supposed to talk to them?" I responded.

"Esther! Why did you come here? Serve them... and talk to them!" she commanded as she shoved the tray into my hands. This time, I allowed myself to look around and see the many faces of need. I placed the tray in front of a man whose eyes showed little hope and whose gnarled hands told me his story. As I looked into his eyes, I said, "Sir, I'm glad you came here today." He reached over, put his hands on mine, and said, "Lady, I'm glad you came today!" After several hours of hard but rewarding work, David and I drove home in silence…each in our own thoughts of the people we met that morning.

My thanks go to Myrtle for reminding me: *If you have some, give some. If you need some, take some. Love that stoops is grace!*

A LEADER TAUGHT ME TO STOOP

Dr. Bob Hamblin was my supervisor when I was on the evangelism staff of the Southern Baptist Home Mission Board, now the North American Mission Board. He told me a story about an experience he had a number of years ago with the Billy Graham Itinerate Evangelism Conference in Amsterdam, Holland.

Dr. Graham had invited a large number of American ministers to attend this conference. As they gathered there to hear his words, Dr. Graham told the Americans that as they had noticed, he had not invited them to be on the platform as speakers. He desired for them to serve the men and women from the third-world countries who had come to this conference for evangelism training. He continued to tell the ministers they were to do the menial things for the conference, such as be in the registration booth, run the welcome center, operate the lost and found, and serve in the cafeteria lines. In other words, he wanted them to be ministers and servants to their brothers and sisters from around the world.

Dr. Hamblin later said to me, "I wondered if Dr. Graham knew who I was. I was vice president of the evangelism section of the Home Mission Board of the Southern Baptist Convention! Why, I had spoken in some powerful pulpits in America."

As the week progressed, the Americans found themselves doing exactly what Dr. Graham had asked them to do—being servants. As Dr. Hamblin continued his story, he said, "As Ruth [Dr. Hamblin's wife] and I served in the food line, we watched the men and women from the third-world countries put sandwiches in each of their pockets. I suppose they thought this might be their food for the week...or perhaps, they were just hungry. I told my wife that we would go across the street to McDonald's so there would be plenty of food left for them."

At the end of the week, Dr. Graham again called the American ministers together. This time, he asked them to go back to their hotels and take out a suit of clothing and be prepared to bring it to the altar to give to a third-world brother in the final service of the conference. When Bob and Ruth got back to their hotel, he said that he was thinking, *"I wonder if Dr. Graham knows where I buy my clothes?"*

He told me that his heart won out, and the last day when the altar call was given, he and his wife made their way to the altar. He laid down one of his suits, as well as a shirt, a tie, and a pair of shoes and socks. His wife also laid down one of her dresses. His next words struck my heart: "For the first time in my life, I understood *real power!*" The Heavenly Father must have smiled over the altar that day, but surely all of heaven applauded for every bent knee rejoicing as the family of God served each other.

I was in Amsterdam speaking some years ago and told this story in my message, only to be surprised again by God. A minister came to me and said he had taken some of the clothes from that altar service, had worn them awhile, and then had given them away to another brother in need!

If you have some, give some. If you need some, take some. Love that stoops is grace!

AN ORGANIZER TAUGHT ME TO STOOP

One week before a fall student conference at which I was to be the speaker, I received a call from the organizer, Dr. Shirley Williams, the director of Baptist Student Ministry in the state of Missouri.

"Esther, we've canceled the student meeting at Windermere Conference Center."

My first thought was that this might mean I would have a weekend at home with my husband. Her next words pierced my heart.

"We've canceled the meeting at the conference center and are moving it into the city of St. Louis. As you know, the rivers have overflowed due to the heavy rains, and mud is everywhere...so we are going to mud out for the flood victims."

With my heart in my throat, I said, "Yes, the church is going to be the church."

Shirley asked if I still wanted to come to the meeting.

"Absolutely, but only if you will let me work alongside the students."

She then told me the shots I'd need to take to protect myself and the clothing I'd need. She said she would supply fireman rubber boots!

I knew the theme for the meeting was "It's your serve!" How like God to set that theme way before the student meeting happened and right when St. Louis needed to see the *stooping love* of Christians. We began Friday night with opening celebration. During the closing of that celebration time, each student was given a white towel, which had written on it these words: *Towels and Basins.*

Saturday morning, more than 600 students were sent out all over St. Louis in teams—with much help from the inner city missionaries—to mud out houses, feed the hungry in food lines, unload truckloads of supplies, and organize supplies in a warehouse. I quietly slipped into the back of a van with about 14 students. They did not recognize me in my fireman clothes. As I worked beside these young people, we mudded out a small African American church and replaced dry wall. The students sang the whole time they worked. As we prepared to leave that church, a number of the church members gathered around and prayed over us.

Our next assignment was a large church. The sanctuary was undamaged, but the basement was in terrible shape. When I looked at the mess down there, my heart sank, wondering what we could possibly do to make a difference. Again, the students sang as they mudded out rooms, cleaned out trash, and painted rooms. Our lunch arrived, courtesy of the Men's Mission Disaster Team. We blessed the food, and no one said a single negative word about the sandwiches without fixings and sodas without ice.

After finishing both churches, our leader sent us out in pairs to find neighbors who might need help, instructing us to share Christ with the people we would meet. In no time, everyone had come back to the church, because we could not find anyone close that needed us. Then two young boys, riding bikes through the flooded intersection, pointed us toward a home across the road. We formed a human chain and walked through the water until we reached the home.

An older gentleman was sitting on the steps of the shell of what was once his home and office. He had been a photographer in the US Army, and in retirement, he still had a studio. We asked if we could help. He shrugged his shoulders. The evidence of the destruction of his home and studio was piled outside his home—higher than the roof. He said the city government would get to it next week. We insisted on cleaning it up ourselves.

I worked with those students as they sang and depleted that pile of trash. They filled two truck-sized dumpsters with the refuse from Leon Ray's home. As I worked along beside them, the Spirit whispered, "Tell him why you came to help."

I walked over to the step and sat down beside Leon. After introductions, he told me his wife was not well and that this tragedy put her in bad shape. His voice was tearful as he told of his travels with the government and all the dignitaries whose pictures he had taken. "It's all lost now," he said.

"Mr. Ray, do you know why these students have come today?"

"I think so," he answered quietly.

"They have come in response to a need in the community because of their personal relationship to Jesus Christ."

He smiled for the first time. He told me that he knew Christ. I told him about the student conference and about the 600 students who had been sent to work throughout St. Louis that day—getting their towels dirty—stooping to serve. I went back to work and noticed that one by one, the students began to go over and sit by Leon to visit with him.

We were almost to the bottom of the pile of soggy rubbish when I pulled out a Bible with a pearl cover; it was still in perfect condition and completely dry. I rushed over to Leon and said, "Look what I found!" I put the Bible in his hands. He smiled a second time.

"This is my wife's Bible and she will be so happy. Maybe this will help her in this rough time." He held it to his heart. I watched as he opened the Bible. Inside the front cover was a baby picture of their only son. He smiled for the third time...through tears. I cried, too.

How gracious of God...to preserve His Word for this family that lost everything they owned. As we wound up our work at Leon's and were about to leave, we gathered in a circle to pray, but before one of us could pray,

Leon asked if he could pray. And pray he did! The students and I walked back across the intersection through the water, but with spirits walking *on* the water.

At the end of that hard day of work, Saturday night's celebration service was electric with joy and excitement. We came to the service dirty from mudding out the houses—but with hearts clean and fresh like a mountain stream. In the closing ceremony, I told the students to come to the altar and put their towels on the nails on the cross if they would be willing to go back to the campuses to serve their fellow students. I stepped away from the podium and was amazed at what I saw...and heard. Students began tearing their towels in half—wanting to keep a reminder of that experience—and bringing the other half of their towels to the cross. What a picture... a cross covered in torn dirty white towels! To these Missouri students, I owe a great debt of gratitude, because they allowed me to serve with them. I have great hope for our nation, because of students willing to be servants.

If you have some, give some. If you need some, take some. Love that stoops is grace!

A CHURCH TAUGHT ME TO STOOP

Frazier Memorial United Methodist Church in Montgomery, Alabama, is a true servant church. Their pastor, Dr. John Ed Mathison, has a passion for freeing the laity to do the work of the ministry. The youth group of the church decided that they were spiritually dead and needed a revival. So...they began revival by having a funeral, burying their old program. They then began to build the program they thought God desired for them. How exciting! Think of other churches that might need to do this with a variety of programs. There could be a lot of funerals.

Their pastor's passion for hands-on mission was the flame that sent these young people out to minister in their own community. I heard John Ed tell what their youth group did when the county fair and circus came to Montgomery. With a new vision for ministry, the young people got together with their leaders and planned a first-class welcome banquet for the circus workers. They received permission and set the time to have the event in one of the circus tents. The tables were set with the best dishes and glasses available, and fresh flowers were on every table.

As the circus workers came into the tent, they each, according to their custom, had their own eating utensils under their arms! The young people presented a short program they had planned for the circus workers; that was a turnaround—those who usually entertain became the audience. The youth expressed gratitude to the circus employees for coming and making their state fair a fun and safe place to be. They presented a long-stemmed rose to each circus worker. Some acted surprised. Some wept. Some expressed thanks, saying nothing like this had ever happened to them. The management of the circus told the church, "We will never forget Montgomery, Alabama."

If you have some, give some. If you need some, take some. Love that stoops is grace!

A GARDENER TAUGHT ME TO STOOP

My friend Karla Worley and I were talking about our gardening habits and joys that come to us because of our gardening. She told me she belongs to a garden club in her neighborhood. I told her I wasn't in a garden club; I just like to putter alone or with Bob in my small garden.

"Oh, we're not the usual garden club," she told me. "We do ministry through our gardens."

"Tell me more."

"Well, first of all, when we work in anyone's garden, we always leave behind a watering can with a scroll of Scripture in it: *'So then neither the one who plants nor the one who waters is anything, but God who causes the growth'* (1 Corinthians 3:7). We do work in each other's garden, but our primary purpose is to do something for other women who happen to be overwhelmed with life at the moment. We do edging, trimming, planting, landscaping, pruning, and leaf raking. We don't just pick flowers, honey, we haul trees! We do have fun together; we talk about our lives, share issues that might be overwhelming us at the moment, and encourage each other. It's a great friendship time. When we hear of someone sick or in need of encouragement, we check to see what each club member has growing, and then we gather the best bouquet and take it to the person in need."

All this time, I thought my garden was for my joy and solitude, and here was this young woman telling me she uses her garden to bless others! Then I remembered my best friend, Jo Vaughn, telling me that one of the great joys of gardening is sharing the produce. Gardening takes much stooping. So does serving, and my friend Karla and her garden club understand that.

If you have some, give some. If you need some, take some. Love that stoops is grace!

A MISSIONARY TAUGHT ME TO STOOP

My friends, John and Ann Faulkner, invited me to come to Nairobi, Kenya, to teach a women's mission retreat for missionary wives. The setting was in beautiful Brackenhurst, high in the mountains.

The first week was a wonderful time of worship and fellowship. After taking a few days' break to see one of the magnificent game parks, we headed back for the second week retreat. The leaders told me I would notice a different atmosphere the second week, as the missionaries from southern Africa are very different. It did not take long to notice the difference. There was such laughter, joy, and fellowship. Living in a war-ravaged area where they are often afraid for their own personal safety and that of their family, they seemed to value every moment of life.

Desiring me to experience what it is like to live in remote areas as they did, they put me in a skit the first night. I was asked to sit in the seat of honor. Then they gave me gifts such as they might receive on the mission field. One live gift, a chicken, was placed directly in my lap—much to my surprise and to the ladies' delight. The chicken was a gift I was happy to give back. Next, they gave me an assignment: Go to the post office. For this part of the program, they had planned all kinds of interruptions that would keep me from getting there—interruptions they encountered daily on their mission fields. A beggar accosted me by grabbing at my clothes. The women laughed as I whipped off my earrings and gave them to the beggar. Another beggar came at me, and I took off my necklace and gave it to her. They laughed even harder. They were having a great time of sport with me. The last time a beggar came, I thought about giving my sweater, but it had huge knitted buttons, so I just pulled down my elastic waist skirt—as if to give it away. (Please know that only women were in this audience!) I had on a black slip under the skirt, so I felt safe. The ladies stood to their feet—screaming and clapping in delight. We laughed until we cried. Later that night, I thought, *Yes, these ladies are different. What a sweet gift from the Father that each group had their own unique fragrance of Christ.*

The day I was to leave, the women had a time of testimony and thanked me for coming to be with them. It was a most humbling experience to be blessed by the body of Christ.

A woman by the name of Kathy stood first and said, "I bless God that Esther came, 'cause I haven't laughed in six months...but when you pretended to take off your skirt for the beggar, I laughed. Even when I got back to my room, I cried and laughed with God until the healing started to come."

The ladies applauded. They knew Kathy's personal story. In their first four years of service, Kathy's family had experienced major sickness and their home had been broken into more than once—enough to make anyone forget how to laugh.

Kathy continued her words, referring to the story I had shared earlier in the week about the Americans giving away their clothes at the Billy Graham meeting, and said through her laughter, "And Esther, if you ever decide to give *your* clothes away, I want that outfit you had on last night—that skirt and sweater." She could not possibly have known that I had just bought that outfit for the trip.

I stood and looked at her—and from my heart these words came forth: "Kathy, I want you to have that outfit!" I sat down, feeling good about my new friend in Christ. I felt such joy. I wasn't even thinking *love that stoops is grace!* I felt like I was ***flying***—not ***stooping***.

After that time of tears and laughter, everyone headed off to lunch in another building. Kathy waited until everyone was gone to speak with me. "I can't take that outfit, but my national pastor and his wife have just had a fire, and she needs clothes. If you like, I will give it to her."

"Fine," I said. Inside my heart, all I could envision were the needs of her pastor's wife and the fat suitcase I was packing earlier that morning in preparation for going home that night.

At lunch that day, one of the missionaries jokingly said to me, "All the tall missionaries have gotten together, and we know what outfits of yours we'd like to have—when you decide to get rid of them. Again, my heart felt a deep impression about my fat suitcase. I went back to the room and unpacked that suitcase, which then left ample room for all the gifts (minus the live chicken, of course) given to me that first night by the women of each country. A shelf in my office now contains those gifts and memories from missionaries in Kenya.

Later that afternoon when I spoke again, I told the group what Kathy had shared with me about her pastor's wife and what God had shown me about my fat suitcase. To their complete surprise, I said, "My clothes are laid out for you at the back of the room. Please help yourself to whatever you need."

Afterward, Kathy came to me and said, "I don't know how to receive very well, but I really would like to have that dress. In the quietness of my room, God reminded me that you gave it to me, and I could receive it." I was so happy, telling her that I really wanted her to have it. We hugged. We cried. Kathy left then.

I went to my last meal with these new friends, knowing how hard it was going to be to say good-bye to the women. We shared more tears. All of a sudden, the room broke out into full laughter and applause as Kathy came into the dining hall with my dress on—accessorized with earrings, necklace, and a big name tag that read *Esther Burroughs*. She walked through the room with the grace of a New York model, to the sounds of her sisters' joyful laughter mixed with tears.

If you have some, give some. If you need some, take some. Love that stoops is grace!

Following the Leader

> *Then he* [Jesus] *told them what they could expect for themselves: "Anyone who intends to come with me has to let me lead. You're not in the driver's seat—I am. Don't run from suffering; embrace it. Follow me and I'll show you how. Self-help is no help at all. Self-sacrifice is the way, my way, to finding yourself, your true self. What good would it do to get everything you want and lose you, the real you?"*
>
> —Luke 9:23–25 (*The Message*)

Being a servant **is not popular.**

　It **is difficult.**

Being a servant **is not fashionable.**

　It matters not whom you serve.

Being a servant **is not easy.**

　It requires humility and earns you little earthly reward.

Being a servant **is not entertaining.**

　It **is entertaining angels unaware.**

Being a servant **is not hard.**

　It **is impossible**—without the Spirit of Christ.

Prayer, prison, persecution, and power identify the New Testament church. No wonder the early church knew the joy of loving each other and having all things in common. Would you say programs, personalities, popularity, and prosperity identify today's church? What if today's church took seriously the Scripture about the poor...the widow...the homeless...the children...the sick...and the dying? Is today's church a servant church? Mission agencies say that the average Evangelical church today spends 99 cents of every dollar on themselves. What if Jesus had said, "I don't do feet?" How would disciples—then and now—know what He expects of us? How would we learn how to serve?

I believe serving begins with one person—just one. Don't say what the church isn't doing. You are the church. You, as an individual, can serve—you can make a difference.

If you have some, give some. If you need some, take some. Love that stoops is grace!

Splashed and Splashing

1. Have you ever experienced a foot-washing service? If so, describe what you felt.
2. When and where was the last time you served someone in your family or in the church family? How did it make you feel?

3. Ask God to show you someone in need. Ask Him how you can be a servant in that particular situation, without revealing who you are. Write the name of that person here. _____

4. The most difficult place to be a servant may be in our own families! Watch for opportunities to serve your husband/wife/children. Begin seeing yourself as a servant, and begin serving. Write down some ways you plan to serve.

5. Mother Teresa was asked why she continued to serve, considering the many she ministered to who died. Her reply was, "I choose to see Christ in the face of every man and every need." How does that make you feel?

More Splashing

Read:

- *The Ragamuffin Gospel,* by Brennan Manning (Sisters, OR: Multnomah Publishers, 2000).

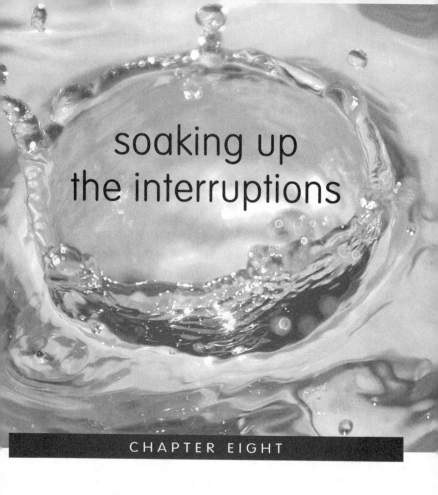

soaking up
the interruptions

Jesus loved life! He invited a fellow out of a tree to play host to Him. He witnessed to those who crossed His path. He ate with sinners...forgave adulterous women... told stories to children...turned water to wine...and changed lives forever. He was focused! His focus was to be about His Father's business as He headed to the cross.

When Jesus was 12 years old, He went to the temple to listen and inquire—while His worried parents looked for Him. When they found Him, He simply said: *"Why is it that you were looking for Me? Did you not know that I had to be in My Father's house?"* (Luke 2:49). During His ministry, He said:

> *"I can do nothing on My own initiative.*
> *As I hear, I judge; and My judgment is just,*
> *because I do not seek My own will, but the*
> *will of Him who sent Me…. But the testimony*
> *which I have is greater than the testimony of*
> *John; for the works which the Father has given*
> *Me to accomplish—the very works that I do—*
> *testify about Me, that the Father has sent Me."*
> —John 5:30,36

He ministered to people—with the weight of the world on His shoulders—and the weight of God's love in His heart. His passion was to do what His Father had sent Him to do.

"For high in the mountains the tiniest brook gave its life to a stream. The streams flowed together and came to the river," say the songwriters Bonnie and Dan Keen. A profound truth, don't you agree? You and I get our life from the river of living water. As we accept the flow from His life to our lives, then we become a river… flowing out to a dry and barren land. Imagine living in such obedience to God that the flow of His love from my life develops a thirst in someone else—a thirst for this thirst-quenching water. How does this happen, you might ask?

Let us begin by looking at typical day in the life of Jesus. You and I live and breathe by our mini notebook computers and pocket calendars, sometimes hoping for no interruptions, whereas Jesus addressed each interruption as God's divine appointment. Think about that: living daily, expecting any interruption to be God's divine appointment. Regarding circumstances in our lives, we perhaps are quick to say, "What a coincidence" or "You won't believe what happened!" Jesus was never surprised by the activity of God. In fact, He only did what the Father told Him to do. No wonder He moved around with such assurance and authority.

Jesus's Divine Encounters

Previously in this book, I referred to the interruptions in our daily lives and how we can use them to *splash the living water.* Let's look at the interruptions in the life of Jesus as found in Matthew chapters 8 and 9. Rather than interruptions, let's called them *divine encounters.*

Jesus climbed a mountain with His disciples, and He taught them all that is recorded in His famous Sermon on the Mount and more. When He came down from the mountain, the crowd followed.

Divine encounter 1. Jesus encountered a leper who bowed down to Him and asked for cleansing. Jesus put forth His hand and touched him. Immediately the leprosy was gone.

Divine encounter 2. Jesus walked to Capernaum and was interrupted by a centurion, who came to Him on behalf of a servant who was critically ill. Jesus embraced this interruption and patiently listened as the Centurion explained the situation: Jesus did not need to come to his home; Jesus needed only to speak a healing word. After marveling at the centurion's great faith, Jesus spoke that word of healing, and when He did, the servant was immediately healed.

Divine encounter 3. Jesus went to Peter's home, where Peter's mother-in-law was lying sick in bed. Jesus touched her hand, and the fever left her. She was even able to get up and minister to Him.

Divine encounter 4. That evening, many demon-possessed persons were brought to Jesus, and He cast out the spirits and healed the sick. Then Jesus told the disciples to get the boat ready to cross the lake.

Divine encounter 5. On the way to the boat, a scribe interrupted Jesus, expressing a desire to follow Him. Jesus patiently explained what kind of life that would be. Can't you just imagine the disciples waiting anxiously as Jesus took His time visiting with this man?

Divine encounter 6. Even before Jesus could get in the boat, another would-be follower expressed a desire to follow Him, but only after he could clear up some family matters. Leaving this man with strong words, a tired Jesus finally got into the boat and fell asleep immediately.

Divine encounter 7. A storm arose. The disciples woke Jesus, begging Him to save them from perishing. Once awake, He questioned their fear and then rebuked the wind and sea. The storm stopped. (I wish I could have seen the disciples' faces when that happened!)

Divine encounter 8. Arriving at the other side of the lake, Jesus was again interrupted—this time by two demon-possessed men who came running toward the boat. He dealt with the men and cast the demons into a herd of pigs, which then charged into the sea and drowned.

Divine encounter 9. Perhaps Jesus was still needing to rest, but the whole town came out to where He was. They were probably upset about losing their pigs, and demanded that Jesus leave their town. Jesus joined the disciples at the boat, and they went back to Capernaum.

Divine encounter 10. Stepping on shore, Jesus saw people bringing a paralytic to Him. He noted their great faith and told the paralytic to take courage because his sins were forgiven. Some of the scribes resented that, and said Jesus was blaspheming, which gave Jesus the opportunity to show His authority. He healed the boy. The multitudes were in awe and glorified God.

Divine encounter 11. As Jesus walked on from there, He saw Matthew, and invited him to become a disciple.

What a day! What an example! Not once did Jesus even inquire about the time of day or complain about all the encounters He had experienced. Consider living in the expectancy of divine encounters and interruptions, in which the Spirit allows the flow of living water to spill and splash out on the people you encounter, drawing others to the well of living water.

My Divine Encounters

Jesus's day was full, much like most any day on my personal calendar or yours, except for the healing events. Well, maybe.

Here's a typical day for me:

Monday morning finds me up early for my quiet time, which may be interrupted by a family member asking for prayer. My prayer group meets from nine until noon. A time of laughter is shared, followed by a time of confession, tears, and concern over situations. After the tearful confessions, loving words are spoken and hearts begin mending. Next comes joy and celebration. Now, I believe that's healing!

These days, my next activity is a workout at a local health spa. Sometimes, I have opportunity to pray with or for a friend. Connecting with women at this place of workout gives opportunity to share encouragement with fellow strugglers.

Next stop is perhaps the frame shop, where I drop off a wedding invitation to be framed as a gift to a special friend to Bob and me. I think of this young bride-to-be and how God has allowed Bob and me to minister in her life. So I say, "Patrick, this has to be beautiful. I want it to be a prayer blessing for this young couple as they start married life." He smiles and says, "Another blessing from you, hey?"

I stop next at my bank to make a deposit. The clerk says to me, "Have a good day!" My response is, "May you have a blessed day." As I drive from the bank, I express thanks to God for the past weekend's speaking engagement, at which the women enriched my life and encouraged my walk with the Father. Because of their gift to me, I will be able to give to others.

My next stop might be the grocery store. As I go through the checkout lane, I punch the debit card machine button—asking for $50 dollars cash back. The young clerk is from Haiti and comments on the arrival of the much-needed rain; I respond, "It is an answer to prayer for sure." She smiles widely and nods, admitting that she has also prayed for rain that would help put out the fires. (At the time of this writing, Florida is virtually on fire!) Our hearts have a knowing exchange. As I walk away, I think to myself, *she is a Christian*. I put the groceries in the car and head for home—in the rain.

Groceries put away, I am heading for a quick nap, which is needed because of the long weekend traveling. But before I can get to the bedroom, the phone rings and my best friend is full of good news about her family vacation. After 45 minutes of love, laughter, and joyful exchanges, we close our phone time by sharing family prayer requests. What would we do without the prayers of each other! No wonder Jesus often invited His disciples to pray with Him.

Like Jesus on the boat, I also get a nap.

Refreshed and with a fresh cup of tea, I sit down at my computer to continue writing this book. I am just getting started when a fax comes that brings another ministry opportunity and causes me to give thanks for God's faithfulness in my speaking ministry. I stop to fax the copy to my capable assistant. I am back to my writing when the doorbell rings. It is a neighbor with whom I had coffee about a week ago. She is bringing me a makeup sample from a new shop in the mall. What a great neighbor! I take a break from writing to edit a manuscript that is due shortly, and just as I finish that assignment, the graphic artist with whom I am working on a newsletter calls. It is a joy to visit with her, because she is so gentle and hears the ideas of my heart as she assists my ministry with her artistic gifts.

Once again, I am back at my desk writing—totally unaware of the time. I hear the garage door opening and know that my sweetheart is home. His arrival signals our daily ritual. He always comes into the kitchen, opens his briefcase, and shares all kinds of good stuff from his day at the office, including email from friends, articles he thinks I will enjoy, and new books. I then share things from my day. We put on our walking clothes and take off for our daily exercise of walking about three miles together. I cherish this time greatly. It is our time to share with each other about our family, work, ideas, and dreams.

In the conversation, I mention that I had just come from the grocery store, and as always, he asks how much I spent on groceries this trip. In that split second, I realize I had left the grocery store without the $50 dollars cash! As soon as we get home, I call the store and give the receipt number to the manager. She calls back in ten minutes and tells me that the money is still in the cash drawer. Thanking God, I get in the car to make yet another trip to the grocery store. I find the young woman who had checked me out. As I come to her counter, she steps out to hug me (it's a woman thing) and thanks me for coming back. I say, "I thank you. I sense that you are a Christian, and I'm grateful for your honesty." She grins and in her beautiful accent, says, "I am! I am!" Back in my car, I thank God again for the short encounter we had about prayer that led us to express our faith.

As I begin dinner preparation, the doorbell rings. Tea towel in hand, I answer the door to discover a huge basket of flowers! Bob and I are celebrating our fortieth anniversary and he has sent a bouquet of flowers every month since January—each bouquet containing exactly 40 stems of flowers. He is home, so I embrace him and express my gratitude for this lovely interruption, which demonstrates his love for me.

After supper, conversation continues, interrupted by a few more phone calls. Then, it's time for bed already!

Does my day sound typical to you? Maybe so—with or without the flowers—and maybe not. Maybe you have different types of work and activities, but are busy all the same. My day, as yours, is full of interruptions, some of which allow us to express our faith and love for Christ. We make the choice about our attitude concerning interruptions. Jesus did, also!

Your Circles of Concern

Several years ago, someone gave me a book by the late Oscar Thompson, *Concentric Circles of Concern*. For many years before his death, Dr. Thompson was a professor at Southwestern Baptist Theological Seminary, Fort Worth, Texas. In preparation for teaching his students about evangelism, he asked God to show him a way to teach them that would change all of eternity. He then studied Jesus in the New Testament and saw His pattern of relationships. Dr. Thompson taught that sharing Christ is about building and repairing relationships. Think about it. All of life is about relationships.

Bitter Relationships
- A child separated from parents
- Family members angry at each other
- Teenage romance breakup
- A friendship damaged by jealousy
- Loss of a spouse or parent
- Divorce

- Loss of a job
- Struggles in the church

Sweet Relationships
- Loving parents
- Laughter from a true friendship
- That first date
- The wedding day
- Friendships at work
- Birth of a child or a grandchild

Good relationships help us to grow to become all that God desires. Unhealthy relationships produce:
- Broken relationships
- Broken homes
- Divided churches
- Weak governments

The book of Acts, referring to disciples, says they went *"from house to house"* sharing Jesus. It happened over and over again in the New Testament—Andrew went to Peter…Philip went to Nathanael…the woman at the well went to her city…Cornelius called in his relatives and close friends…the Philippian jailer, his household (and this household included servants as well as family members). It is no different today. When someone comes to know the saving grace of the cross, they want to tell others who are dear to them about this miracle in their lives. We make a mistake when we limit our thoughts of evangelism to sharing Jesus just with persons we do not know. Doesn't it make sense to share the good news first with those you do know and about whom you care?

In his book, Dr. Oscar Thompson provides the seven circles of influence in the lives of every person:

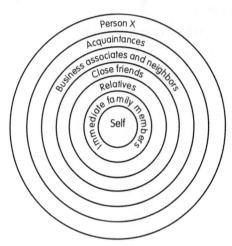

Did you notice that there are seven circles? And there are seven days of the week. Begin the week by praying for yourself, and each day thereafter, move out with a flow of prayer for persons in your circles of concern. You will want to update your list regularly as your circles of concern change with life circumstances. By praying for those in your circles of concern, you will be sensitive to meeting needs in love. When I began praying over my circles of concern, I listed on a page in my prayer journal the persons I was praying for in each circle. It is a wonderful way to pray for those in your life!

Once again, may I say, out of the inflow comes the outflow...gained from our quiet time of worship with the Father. You have, no doubt, met people whose lives just seem to overflow with the love of God. Passing them feels like refreshment from a flowing river. Jesus desires for His love to fill us and flow out of us… touching the world. Paul prayed for the Ephesians to experience that fullness of God: *"To know the love of Christ which surpasses knowledge, that you may be filled up to all the fullness of God"* (Ephesians 3:19). I like *The Message* paraphrase of Paul's prayer: *"You'll be able to take in with all Christians the extravagant dimensions of Christ's love. Reach out and experience the breadth! Test its length! Plumb the depths! Rise to the heights! Live full lives, full in the fullness of God"* (Ephesians 3:18–19 *The Message*).

Are you filled, or are you thirsty? Jesus tells the thirsty what to do about it and what the results will be: *"If anyone thirsts, let him come to me and drink. Rivers of living water will brim and spill out of the depths of anyone who believes in me this way"* (John 7:37–38 *The Message*).

The evidence of the fullness of the presence of the Holy Spirit in our lives is directly related to the outflow. *If there is a filling, there is going to be a flowing. If there is no outflow, you can be sure there is no filling.* Obedience and joy are inextricably joined together. **Obedience**—taking time to develop a river by drinking up the riches of Christ Jesus—brings *joy*—taking time for every encounter sent by God and sharing from the overflow of the river of life in Christ.

In living in the fullness of God, we are aware of our influence and always look for opportunities for building bridges to relationships—in times of joy and in times of sorrow—which allow us to provide that flow of living water. The concept that Dr. Thompson shared is so profound, yet very simple.

The Ripples Spread

Have you ever thrown a rock into a lake and watched the ripples spread out from the center, where the rock had dropped out of sight? As you continued to throw more rocks, you may have noticed the circles spreading out and beginning to overlap each other. That beautiful concept works in personal relationships. As our *circles of influence* go out...touching other persons in their circles of influence, we can live in expectancy of what the power of the Holy Spirit will do to draw even more people to Jesus.

In class one day, Dr. Thompson said, "God holds us responsible for every person who comes into our circle of influence." He continued by saying, "Some of them are cantankerous, some of them don't like you, and some of them you don't want to love. They are there for you to love—to meet their needs—to draw them to Jesus."

"Dr. Thompson," a student named Jim spoke up. "I have all kinds of trouble with that. You don't understand my situation. You grew up in a Christian home. But my father abandoned my mother and me 26 and a half years ago. I am 27 years old. I have never seen him. I do not want to see him." At that intense moment, Dr. Thompson prayed for the wisdom of God. He then wrote his translation of Matthew 6:14–15 on the board. "Because of the love of Jesus and His forgiveness in my life, I must be ready to forgive if I am to be forgiven."

Tears rolled down the cheeks of the student. "What must I do? I do not know where my father is. He may not even be alive."

The class immediately went to prayer. Weeks passed. One morning, Jim came into the class and said, "I have something to say to the class, sir. Last night, I received two phone calls. The first came from my mom, saying that one of my aunts had gone to be with the Lord. I thought she was my mother's sister but learned she was my father's sister. At 11:00, I received a second call, and a voice on the other end said, 'Jim? Son? Although I have no right to call you son. But I have heard that you are in seminary preparing for the ministry. I thought you would like to know that I recently gave my life to Jesus Christ. Can you forgive me for what I have done?'" After a pause, Jim continued, "When I could quit sobbing, we talked. We spent an hour on the phone."

Jesus said that *"He who believes in Me…from his innermost being will flow* [gushing up, springing out, flowing over] *rivers of living water"* (John 7:37–38). The flow of the Spirit is like a well that flows with rippling effects on those around us.

Leave a Jar for Someone

I heard a pastor preach from the John 4 text (Samaritan woman at the well), using a hand pump in illustration.

It was an old hand pump, like those used on farms in the 1930s. He demonstrated pumping the handle and showed us the suction cup, bound by a leather washer, that had to be wet to cause suction as the handle was pumped. The combination of pumping and suction drew water up from the well to pour out through the spout.

After his demonstration, he told an interesting story. One of the most unusual messages he had ever seen was related to a hand pump like the one he showed us. The message was scribbled on a scrap of wrapping paper that had been folded and stuffed into a baking powder can, which was then wired to an old well hand pump. That pump offered the only chance of water on a seldom-used trail in California's Mojave Desert. The message read:

> This pump is all right as of June 1932. I put a new sucker washer in it, and it oughta last five years. But the washer dries out and the pump has got to be primed. Under the white rock, I buried a jar of water, out of the sun and cork end up. There's enough water to prime this pump—but not enough if you drink some first. Pour in about a quarter of it and let her soak to wet the leather. Then pour in the rest and pump like crazy. You'll git water. The well never has run dry. But when you git watered up, fill the jar again, and put it like you found it for the next feller.
>
> —Desert Pete

Who left a water jar for you? Imagine where you would be today if it were not for the ripple effect of God's living water.

Take a drink.

Fill the jar.

Pass it on.

Let the flow continue.

What might happen in your community if you concentrated on sharing Jesus with persons in your circles of influence and not so much with perfect strangers? Most people have no trouble speaking to persons in their circles of influence.

Let us take a journey through stories relating to all seven circles and see if we can make a clear presentation of the powerful influence each one of us can be as we choose to relate to our sphere of influence. The premise is this: Love is meeting needs—and when you meet needs, you will have opportunities to share Jesus.

Self

The first circle of influence you have is *yourself*. There is a flow to life. This living water must flow to us first, and then, through us. When Jesus calls us to follow, He calls us to die to self—to *me*, *my*, and *mine*—and to let Him be Lord of our lives. The vertical relationship between you and the Father is most important. When the daily vertical relationship between the Christian and the Father is sweet, fresh, and growing, then horizontal relationships are better and best. It is nearly impossible to be the vessel through which the living water flows when we are out of sorts with self or with others. The water can't get through. I know. I've been there! Love cannot flow through selfishness, hate, greed, insecurity, or anything else that separates us from the fragrance of Christ. That is why it is critical to keep a balance in life and drink in the living water daily. It is only as we drink in that we have something to pour out.

David, a man after God's own heart, cried out, *"Create in me a clean heart, O God, and renew a steadfast spirit within me"* (Psalm 51:10). Make this your prayer: "Lord, cleanse me and flow through me to my circles of concern." Think of the vertical relationship—the renewing—as a process, a literally never-ending process.

Family

After being diligent to keep self in balance, we move to the second circle of influence: *immediate family* (those who live under your roof). For me today, that would be my husband Bob. This circle sometimes includes extended family: parents, returning children, and, in some households, grandchildren. It seems easier for some of us to try to meet the needs in China than to take care of persons in our own homes, which is the very basis for building relationships. This is the most exciting area—and the hardest. People in the immediate family know best our strengths *and* weaknesses and even what buttons to push. They have our number, and they call it often, and usually at the worst times! We must be real at home. What other place can we go where we treat people the worst and still receive love? Nowhere!

When Melody was four years of age, she said to me on the way home from a long day at church and after I yelled at her: "Mommy, how come at church you smile and talk so nice to everyone and you talk so ugly to me and David?" Ouch! See what I mean? Showing love in the family can be difficult at times.

If any one thing could make a difference in the family, I believe it would be improving the art of listening—not *selective* listening or *interruptive* listening, but *heart* listening. Heart listening is difficult because it takes more time than interruptive listening. I was rolling out bread dough one afternoon, up to my elbows in flour, when my son, David, a second grader, sat nearby eating an afternoon snack and telling me the events of the day. I heard him say, rather exasperated, "Look at me when you listen, Mother!" I did that day.

David gave me another lesson in listening in 1980. In March of that year, I took a position with the Southern Baptist Home Mission Board, which is now called the North American Mission Board. I commuted between Birmingham and Atlanta for six months while Melody finished her senior year of high school, David, his ninth grade in junior high, and Bob, his final semester of teaching music at Samford University.

It was a difficult time for me. I had to learn a new city, learn a new ministry, and live alone during the weekdays. I was really homesick in the second month at work. I drove home on a Thursday afternoon instead of Friday to surprise my family. I planned my trip so that I could get to Birmingham in time to pick up David from school, and I was there on time. When I saw him come out of the building, I honked the car horn, which was loud enough for the whole world to hear. I saw his head come up. He knew that horn! He began running toward me. I got out of the car just in time to be picked up and swung around by my ninth grade son! We hugged and hugged. As I got back in the car, I began to cry.

"What's wrong, Mom? You're home! What's the matter?"

"I get so lonely all week by myself in Atlanta," I responded through my tears. "I really miss you and Dad and Mel."

I thought he would say, "We miss you too, Mom!" —but he didn't. He got real quiet. Finally he spoke.

"Mom, when you get home every weekend, you just talk and talk about everything going on in your work and all the people you meet and see. Dad really misses you so much. Dad is so sad with you gone. It's like he's dead or something, and he's no fun at all!"

Whoa! Not only was I not listening, I was talking fast and loud—so Bob would not know how frightened and alone I was. I thought if I pretended I was OK, he wouldn't worry about me so much. I had no idea that it was having the opposite effect on him. Once again, my child taught me about listening...listening with the heart. I believe that type of listening requires eye contact as well as heart and ear contact. You can be sure I got his message. I got home, farmed out the kids, and had Bob all to myself all evening. That night, I was honest with

Bob. Well, we both were honest about our real feelings and fears. What great freedom! That gave us the power to cope with the next months before the family finally moved to Atlanta.

Heart listening helps you discern the need and *love* listening helps draw you to meet some needs so you can be the love of Christ. A woman in Dr. Thompson's class was challenged by the teacher's words that meeting needs leads to being the presence of Christ. As she returned home from class, all set to meet needs in love, she encountered a sink full of dirty dishes, clothes all over the floor, and her husband sitting, feet propped up on the furniture and totally engrossed in the paper. Her instinct was to go on a rampage! Ever been there?

With Dr. Thompson's words fresh in her heart, she greeted everyone kindly, began to pick up the mess in the kitchen, and asked her husband if he would be so kind as to start the bath water for the children while she did the dishes. She heard the water running and then the voices of laughter. By the time she finished her job, she discovered her husband had bathed the children and had them ready for bed. She told Dr. Thompson the next day, "It works! It really works." When you meet needs in love, you are sharing Christ.

Imagine the difference we can make in our family when we realize our circle of influence has the possibility of bearing fruit that remains. In John 15:16, Jesus talks about bearing fruit that remains: *"You did not choose Me but I chose you, and appointed you that you would go and bear fruit, and that your fruit would remain, so that whatever you ask of the Father in My name He may give to you."*

Consider this as a divine appointment: ***you are chosen to bear fruit that remains.*** What a great invitation—to join Christ in Kingdom work. Consider this a promise: You have authority to use His name in prayer for those encounters in everyday family situations. When children see their mother make a sacrificial decision in their behalf, they have seen Christ's love. When a wife hears a husband pray over making difficult extended family choices, she sees Christ's love. When children see parents expressing tenderness toward each other, disciplining in love, working together as a family unit, they see Christ's love as needs are met. Cherish the circle of family in prayer, and open your heart to seeing all God can do in your family.

An area of great interest to me is that of parents praying for the salvation of their children. Please do not leave this responsibility to the church! It is the responsibility—and privilege—of the parents. Today, as a grandmother, my circle has grown, as now I pray that my grandchildren will come to know Christ.

Relatives

The next circle of concern is for *relatives*. That circle can be difficult to deal with, too—like immediate family. It might be difficult because we may not live close enough to visit and have daily influence. It might be difficult because we may live too close, and they know all about us! We can pray that God will give us opportunity to be Christ to those close by and to share Christ with those far away. Consider the task given to us in Acts 1:8 as a divine assignment: *"You will receive power when the Holy Spirit has come upon you; and you shall be My witnesses both in Jerusalem, and in all Judea and Samaria, and even to the remotest part of the earth."*

Think of this verse in the context of family, neighborhood, city, state, country, and the world. To meet the needs of relatives in love, we must think about the widening circle—rippling out from us—touching those we seldom see or meet personally, but trusting the Holy Spirit's power through the family of God showing love in circles of need.

When I was a small child, my favorite uncle, Peter, was in the Royal Canadian Navy. He looked so handsome in his white middy uniform and sailor hat. I was quite sure that when I grew up, I would marry him. While at my grandmother's home one summer, my cousin and I waited each day for him to come home. We never knew the exact day, so while we waited we would swing on the garden gate for a portion of each day. When we saw him coming up the alley, off we would go. After hugs and kisses, he would make us close our eyes while he took our gifts from his pocket and put them behind his back. We then went through the ritual of guessing which hand held the gift. Little did we suspect that whichever hand we chose, there was always a gift!

When I became acquainted with the circle concept, I began a family search to discover if all my relatives knew Christ. I assumed that there would be few who did not know Christ as their personal Savior, but I was amazed at how many did not know Christ!

I then began talking with my mother and praying with her about her brother, my uncle Peter, who did not know Christ. I came under such conviction that I was traveling around the world speaking to women on the subject of lifestyle evangelism and had an uncle who did not know Christ. First, I began to pray. I asked God what could I possibly do, since Peter lived in Toronto, Canada, and I had not seen him in years and had kept up with him only through Christmas cards. The Spirit whispered to me: "Write a letter."

I had just finished reading Gary Chapman's book, *The Five Love Languages*, which shows the reader how to communicate in word pictures that conjure up memories to help bring greater communication between persons. The ripple effect discussed earlier came to mind at just the right time to reshape my thinking about how to write the letter. I wrote about the great days at my grand-mother's house as a child—the picket fence…the swing …the cinder sidewalk…the outhouse, complete with the Sears catalog toilet tissue! I recounted the story of meeting Uncle Peter and receiving his gifts. After refreshing his memory about my childhood memory, I said that I was sorry it had taken so long for me share with him one of the most important gifts that was ever given to me and all mankind—God's love through His Son Jesus.

I wrote out for him the Roman Road to salvation verses. At the end, I offered him the gift that Jesus gives, wrote out a prayer to pray to receive Christ, and invited him to pray that prayer. I sent the letter—covered in my prayers. I did not hear from him for months and months, but I kept on praying.

Later when I went to Glorieta, New Mexico, to speak for a conference, I carried with me some accumulated mail from home. As I was opening one item, a letter from my mother, out dropped a letter written to her. As best I could make out, someone's relative had died. I called my mother to ask from whom this letter had come. It was from my aunt, my mother's sister. Uncle Peter had died. I cried out, "Oh, no!" Mother quickly interrupted, "It's alright. Your Aunt Tootsie has been praying with us for his salvation, and she flew to Toronto to make one last visit to Peter knowing he was very ill. When she knocked on the door and was let in to his room, she stated the purpose of her visit. He quietly responded, 'That is all settled. I got a letter from Esther.'"

That ripple effect took years. My preacher father had shared the plan of salvation with Peter more than once, but he had not been ready those times. My grandmother, mother, and her sister had prayed for him for years. I joined in prayer—late in the process. God used two authors, Oscar Thompson and Gary Chapman, to bring me to the place of obedience to write the letter. The Holy Spirit managed all those circumstances to bring Peter to Himself. Won't we have a party in heaven—celebrating a homecoming? Keep praying.

Our challenge is to flow, flow to the River, and from that river, there will be an outflowing in our circles of influence.

Friends

The next circle of concern includes *friends*. It is easy to be in a relationship and talk about absolutely everything...except Jesus. Your friends have been put in your circle for a reason. When you meet people's needs through shared friendship, you will also have a chance to share Jesus.

I think often of my son's influence on a new friend when he was a student at the University of South Carolina. He quickly became involved in a campus ministry group. His freshman roommate, Jim, was not interested in going with him to the center. David noticed that his roommate had a Bible, but did not know if he knew Christ, so he asked us to pray that he would live Christ in front of Jim. As they got acquainted, Jim confessed his loneliness. David said that he was going to Bible study that night and had met some really great new friends. "Why don't you join me?" Not long into the first semester, those campus ministry friends led Jim to Christ. We watched him grow and mature in the faith. He later became the campus ministry president and now is serving as a pastor, continuing that ripple effect of meeting needs in Christ's love.

Business Associates and Neighbors

The circle continues to move outward, and the next wave flows over *business associates and neighbors*. It is still difficult for me to relate this next story, because it was a painful lesson for me. When Bob and I lived in Abilene, Texas, we had just purchased a home on a little lake—well, since it was in west Texas, maybe it was more like a pond. We had not even had time to paint or change the carpet when the call came for my husband to consider a position on the music faculty as composer-in-residence at Samford University in Birmingham, Alabama. As God directed, we loaded up the cars and began the journey across country. We stopped that first night at an International House of Pancakes, because the children would always eat pancakes. During the meal, Bob said to me, "Did you notice that none of our neighbors came to say good-bye to us?"

I laughed saying, "Well, George said he would miss David always retrieving his dog from their yard."

Finally at a motel, everyone was in bed and asleep—but me. I heard over and over again the words of my husband about our neighbors not saying good-bye to us. I spent the late night hours explaining to God why. I rationalized that we had only lived in that house for four months. I rationalized that we were busy with our small children and many church activities. After all, didn't they see us go out every Sunday with Bibles and Sunday school lesson books in our hands? That must have counted for something! And every Sunday night, we left for church with our discipleship materials in tow.

If they didn't get that, then surely they saw us pack up at 4:00 P.M. every Wednesday—heading out to children's choir, mission group, church supper, teachers' meeting, prayer meeting and choir! Certainly, we had left an impression about our lives on our neighbors!

The next morning at breakfast, I said to my husband, "I know why."

"You know why what?" He responded. Isn't that like a man—they never stay with a woman's train of thought!

"Why our neighbors didn't say good-bye to us," I continued.

"Why?"

"Because we never said hello." You can mark it down. From that moment until now, our neighbors have known who we are...and whose we are!

I have come to believe that you do not live in your house because you like the shutters, though I hope you do. Think *kingdom* for a moment. Think *circle of influence*. What does God desire to do through the flow of His love in your life to meet needs in your neighborhood or office with the possibility of drawing someone to Himself?

A friend of mine in Atlanta walks around her neighborhood, praying over the mailboxes as she passes by. When she sees a moving van, she brings homemade soup, introduces herself, and offers assistance. She has had the privilege of leading some of her neighbors to Christ—just by meeting needs in love.

The workplace takes much of our time; there, we are in another circle of concern. As you have lunch, exercise, or attend staff meetings, you have an opportunity to listen for needs, so you can share His love.

Christ calls us to Himself in creation, making us that singular, particular fragrance of Himself. The love He pours into us will splash out and be such a sweet fragrance that those in our circle will be drawn to Him and, perhaps, receive the gift of salvation. Being a witness is not about a memorized presentation; it is about a personal relationship. A great part of *splashing the living water* that I believe the body of Christ misses is simply talking about the Lord and His reality in our everyday living.

Von serves us at our Saturday morning coffee spot. Her nametag reads, "God is good. Have a blessed day." With the simple statements on her nametag, she has blessed God, spoken His name—which is above every name—and possibly refreshed another member of the body or made someone thirsty for the "love" she is advertising. That is part of our responsibility as Christians—to live in such a way that we make the unbeliever thirsty for the living water in us.

After I broke my arm in a skiing accident, I had to go often to the doctor's office for neuromuscular therapy. It was not long until I became acquainted with the receptionist and shared my calling as a Christian speaker—only to discover she, too, was a Christian. With each visit, I answered the doctor's questions about my ministry, and I shared my faith with him. Later, another nurse joined the staff, and she was also a Christian. In our ordinary conversations, we shared and told each other about our prayer requests from time to time. All three of us began to pray specifically for the doctor.

I moved away from the city, but two years later, I received a phone call from the doctor, telling me that he had become a Christian. He didn't even let me ask about it. He just spilled it out. He asked his receptionist, whom he knew was a Christian, if she thought he was a Christian. She replied that she didn't think so because she made some inquiries to which he did not respond. He pondered her words. The next week, he asked another Christian patient if she thought he was a Christian. She not only told him no, but she gave him the same comments! He then called another patient who knew Christ and asked her to come in and lead him to Christ. Our circles overlapped in meeting needs and in prayer—allowing God's Spirit to draw the doctor to Himself. How exciting it is to know that you are living with the expectancy of being part of God's divine interruptions!

The story is told of a foreign missionary who moved into a national neighborhood, only to be abused by the locals—abused, that is, until there was a water shortage, and the missionary had the only active well in the community. The missionary saw the need and met the need in love by sharing the well and inviting the rock-throwing nationals to come and get needed water.

A church in Colorado has become known for meeting needs of their community. Their premise is that every part of the body gives their gifts to the body in their unique giftedness. One group began a supper club. One couple would clean their home, another couple would prepare and bring the meal, and a third couple would serve as official hosts, making sure everyone was acquainted and comfortable. Each of these couples would invite another couple from the neighborhood or workplace with the plan of sharing their relationship with Christ—not through a prepared presentation but in natural conversation. This activity took place three to four times during the year, and then the church would host a special dinner evening—complete with a guest speaker and a musician. The supper club group would invite their neighbors and business associates one more time to be their guests to the special event. At the end of this evening, there would be a simple, creative presentation of the gospel. The first year's event saw 80 people come to know Christ, because the flow of the river of living water that had been experienced through hospitality.

Acquaintances

The ripples now move us to the circle of *acquaintances*. The dictionary says of the word *acquaintance*, "one you know slightly." Perhaps, this is the widest area in the ripple effect. Everyday, our lives move us among our acquaintances found in the grocery store...the airport... the PTA...the doctor's office...the neighborhood...the beauty salon...the bank...your favorite restaurant...Little League ball games...the swim club...and maybe even church!

Some time ago I boarded an early morning flight out of my city, and as I sat down next to a lady, she was already enjoying her orange juice. I said, "Good morning."

"It is," she responded, "especially if you like what you do."

"You must," I said.

She smiled and nodded.

I inquired, "Is this your home?"

She shared that she was visiting family and was on business.

When the plane was airborne, I inquired about her family and she asked about mine. Later in the conversation I asked, "What is your business that you enjoy so much?" She went into great detail about her work with health care issues for women. We were off and running with an easy conversation. She asked where I was headed. "Out West to speak to a women's retreat." I told her I spoke to women about spiritual health issues. I shared with her my speaking theme and Scripture and a story I was using to begin my talk (probably one of my favorite stories).

She grabbed my arm, and said, "I can't believe this! You won't believe this!" She reached into her purse and pulled out a Peace with God tract. "Last week on this same flight, a man sitting next to me shared the same things you are saying. You don't think this is a coincidence, do you?"

You and I, clothed in the Holy Spirit, have His power in us to draw others to Christ—like *holy magnetism*.

On that plane that morning, I was able to turn a conversation about women's health issues to spiritual health issues, and the Holy Spirit reminded my acquaintance of the little tract in her purse, given to her by someone else. I didn't tell her, but I was super fired up that another Christian was being obedient in his circles of influence and that the Holy Spirit gave me an opportunity to be obedient in my circle.

Do you remember the story about when Jesus was walking through the crowd and a woman reached out in faith to touch just the hem of His garment? When He asked, *"Who touched My garments?"* (Mark 5:30), the disciples said, "Teacher, how could You possibly know in a crowd like this?" (author's paraphrase). The answer to that question is power-packed: *He perceived power going forth from Him.*

Have you ever experienced that? Being obedient to the Father, He chooses to use you, and His power changes lives because of your touch. You will feel His power in the situation—which reminds you that it is His power in you—on loan. It will humble you and, at the same time, energize you in His love.

Max Lucado, in his book *Next Door Savior*, tells the story of a single mom with a frail baby living in a small Arkansas community. Her neighbor would stop by every few days and keep the child so she could shop or rest. After some weeks, her neighbor shared more about her faith, and the woman did what Matthew did. She followed Christ. The friends of the young woman objected. "Do you know what those people teach?" they contested.

"Here is what I know," she told them. "They held my baby." I think Jesus likes that kind of answer, don't you?

During a trip to Europe with a singing group, Bob and I decided we would take the opportunity to travel in France from Lyon to Paris by the bullet train, while the choir traveled by bus. We wanted to have the experience, and we were told we would get to Paris several hours ahead of the group and could get the hotel arrangements and keys ready for their arrival. We said good-bye to the group at the buses and walked to the train station—only to discover the bullet train we needed did not run on Saturdays! The next one would be in two hours. Since we didn't speak French, someone took us to the Travelers Aid waiting room. While sitting there waiting, I noticed a small, demure lady, working quietly behind the desk.

Soon an older woman and a much younger woman entered the room, both crying softly. Their apparel indicated to me that they were from India. The woman came from behind the desk to assist them. It was obvious she could not speak their language, but the hand motions of the two women told that they had been robbed. In frustration, the Travelers Aid attendant got them settled and gave them coffee. Then, she left the room. It was not long before she returned with a train station worker from India who could speak the Indian language. Oh, the joy in their eyes as they heard their own language being spoken. Through tears, they told the story of stolen money and train tickets. I watched as the young man carefully listened to the story and calmly assured them that he would return. He left the room.

The Travelers Aid attendant continued to attend to their needs as best she could. Her presence could be felt as she ministered to the troubled ladies. Soon, the young man came back into the room—quietly confident. In his hands were two new tickets and money for the journey. The tears...the touching...and the bowing were a sight to behold. He then took them to their train stop. I was amazed. A total stranger who happened to be from the same country took care of these women...just because they were from the same country!

What a portrayal of the gospel that was for me. What a picture of the cross. We come totally lost and unworthy and with nothing to our name. Jesus takes our lostness and makes it His. He takes His worthiness and makes it ours. He takes His home and makes it ours...for eternity. Hallelujah! What a Savior!

I was so curious about this Travelers Aid attendant in Lyon, France. She could speak a little English, but I knew no French. I had tried to help her assist the ladies by sitting with them as she went for help. After the ladies had left the room, I inquired, as best I could with my words and hands, about her volunteer work. I told her I also worked with volunteers, placing them in helping ministries in my country.

She told me her story: the death of an only child. The agony and pain of the experience was still evident on her face. She said, "Finally one day, I knew I had to do something to get rid of my pain. I decided I needed to help someone else with life. I came here seven years ago, and I've been here ever since. The only time my pain leaves me is when I am serving here."

Jesus, our wounded healer, calls us to meet needs even through our own pain...to meet needs in His love...to bring hope to others and to ourselves. What a great mission!

Person X

We are now at the concentric circle of *person X*. The concept of the concentric circles is this: If each Christian is obedient in his or her seven circles of concern, there might never be a person X. The overwhelming awe I first felt about the circle concept was the awareness that as the circles fan out, they interact with other circles, and the Holy Spirit is the manager of these interacting situations. I may board an airplane and think I am sitting next to person X, but that person may be your neighbor or acquaintance! Let me illustrate.

Early in the ministry of my father, he would journey every two months into the North Country of Canada to a little village, called Chinook Cove, which was a German farming community. He would preach in the schoolhouse for those who would come to the service. We visited often with the Schmidt family, who lived in that community. My father had led some in that family to know Christ as personal Savior. He had baptized a young man named Allen Schmidt.

Many years later, after completing college and seminary and serving as a pastor in Canada, Allen

Schmidt became the executive director of the Canadian Southern Baptist Convention. Allen has recently retired. It has been my privilege to work with Allen and his wife, Katherine, many times in ministry. In 1988, I was making a videotape series related to lifestyle evangelism. I had asked several churches in the area to send women who would be willing to be the audience for this live taping session. In one of the sessions, I asked my audience to turn to their neighbor and share their story of coming to know Christ.

At the lunch break, a beautiful young woman named Sheryalyn approached me. She said that when she came to know Christ, her pastor in Canada asked her to write her name on a piece of paper. Then he asked her to put it in his hands. He closed his hands and asked her to try and get her name out of his hands. She could not. He then told her that no one could ever take her out of Jesus's hand—ever. I thought that was an excellent illustration. Because of my Canadian heritage, I was curious about her pastor, so I asked her the name of her pastor, and she said, "Allen Schmidt."

I began jumping up and down with excitement. I told her, "When Allen was a teenager, my father was his pastor."

A rush of emotions flooded our hearts as we both realized this was a wonderful example of the flow of God's love through the circles of concern. My father was faithful in his circle. Allen was faithful in his circle. I was being faithful in my circle as I trained others to meet needs with God's love, and the circles' rippling effect would continue as Sheryalyn's life flows out meeting needs and teaching others.

Allow me one more personal illustration. I asked Caroline, my 14-year-old granddaughter, to share about her mission trip this past summer. She emailed me this note:

> I went on a mission trip with my youth group to Chattanooga, Tennessee. We were working with an organization called Widows Harvest Ministries fixing up houses for widows. Several different churches were on the trip, and our work groups were mixed up among the churches. During free time, our youth group hung out together and played games and stuff. We invited some kids from other churches to swim and play volleyball with us on the first day, and for the rest of the week, a girl named Owen hung out with the kids from our church. On the last day, they had a time that if you wanted to, you could get up and talk about your experiences on the trip. Owen got up and said that our church had shown her that being a Christian is hard, but it can also be really fun and that the Bible isn't just a book of rules to prevent you from having fun. She said that our example showed her how to live for Christ in all you do. She accepted Christ and told us that she couldn't wait to go home and tell her friends about the joy of Christ. I love you Nana! I hope this is good enough.
>
> —Caroline

Yes, precious granddaughter Caroline, this is good enough...sharing Jesus is always good enough!

During the summer of 2004, Caroline's father and her older sister, Anna, went on a mission trip to Metamoros,

Mexico, with their church. Late in the week, the teams were sent to prayerwalk the community and follow God's leadership in knocking on doors and visiting people on the sidewalks of the community. Anna and her father both had the joy of leading persons to Christ. You can imagine my delight as I heard these precious granddaughters tell their experiences of seeing someone come to know Jesus Christ. A citizen of God's kingdom is like a river about to spill over its banks...simply *splashing the living water.*

Where do your circles of concern take you, and how do you view each encounter? The real miracle here is that an encounter with life could bring life for another because of the cross. How could we do less than our best in every encounter—thinking kingdom living and splashing the living water on every encounter that is put before us!

Splashed and Splashing

Probe: My prayer is that this chapter has made you look with new eyes at your circles of influence. The Holy Spirit will show you opportunities. You can begin by making a small circle for self, and add six more concentric circles, each one larger than the last. List the concern of each circle...or add names in each area of concern listed below. As you add names, remember these are people already in your circle of influence. Some already know Christ, some need prayer, some need a closer walk with God, and some do not know Christ.

1. *Self* _____

2. *Family* _____

3. *Relatives* _____

4. *Close friends* _____

5. *Neighbors/business associates* _____

6. *Acquaintances* _____

7. *Person X* _____

Begin by praying for each person in your circles of concern. Pray for...

Sunday	...yourself.
Monday	...your family.
Tuesday	...your relatives.
Wednesday	...close friends.
Thursday	...neighbors and business associates.
Friday	...acquaintances.
Saturday	...person X.

You may want to keep this list handy in your prayer journal for continual updates.

More Splashing

Read:

- *Concentric Circles of Concern*, by W. Oscar Thompson, W. Oscar Thompson, Jr., Carolyn T. Ritzmann, and Claude V. King (Nashville: Broadman & Holman, 1999).

splashing the living water

Some time ago, I was flying from Dallas to Knoxville with the usual change of planes in Atlanta. When it was time for my connecting plane to depart Atlanta, we were still in the air—circling the airport because of bad weather. I *had* to make my connection. I said to the stewardess, "I must get off this plane!" I don't know what I thought she might do. Perhaps open a door and let me off?

She calmed me by saying that my connecting plane to Knoxville was probably circling Atlanta also, and she gave me instructions to follow as soon as we landed. When the door opened, I rushed off the plane, following her instructions, and sure enough, there was a car waiting for me at the bottom of the steps! Once I was in the car, it proceeded to drive me under the bellies of all those huge planes—from concourse A to concourse D—to allow me to make my connecting flight. (The airlines do not provide this courtesy in today's travel, I'm sorry to say.) As soon as I stepped inside the cabin, the door was shut and the plane was cleared for departure. I found my 10-C seat and sat down. As I buckled up, I quietly said, "Thank you, Father!"

The young man sitting next to me looked my way and said, "Excuse me. Were you talking to me?"

"Oh no, sir. I was thanking God that I made this flight connection." Still out of breath from the hurried connection, I explained the reason for my expression of thanks: "I am to speak in a Knoxville church in the morning at 8:30 and again at 11:00. I'm also scheduled in another church tomorrow evening and yet another on Monday morning."

He looked at me in puzzlement and said, "What are you...a nun or something?"

I laughed and replied, "Oh no! I'm a priest!"

I can still see him looking at my collar...or at least looking *for* my collar. I didn't say that flippantly— I believe all Christians are priests.

"I could use a priest," he said.

Isn't that just like God—to outdo Himself that evening, allowing me to make the connection for this divine encounter...just so He could bring glory to Himself by allowing me to minister to this hurting young man! This husband and father began his "confession" before the plane even got in the air. He told me that he was going through a divorce and that he had small children who needed him. The hurt came pouring forth from his heart, as did the tears from his eyes.

I patiently listened as he told of trying to get ahead in business, sadly, to the neglect of family and church. He wanted me to tell him what he could do to recapture his marriage and home. (I believe God uses my grand-mother status to attract and encourage younger folk. I just love being a grandmother!)

In the telling of his story, he responded to my questions concerning his faith background. He shared that he had grown up in church, had attended Bible study, and knew Christ, but had gotten away from the church. I shared with him my faith journey and encouraged him to go back to church and ask for help there. He said he would do that, and I said I would remember him in prayer...praying that God's love would invade his circumstances in such a way as to bring healing in his family.

After our short flight, he said, "I'm so glad you made this plane and sat next to me. I don't think it was an accident."

"Nor do I," I responded with a rejoicing heart for God's kindness in allowing this young man to enter my *circle of influence.* I am convinced that our world needs more priests—not more pastors! As 1 Peter 2:9 reminds us, *"You are a chosen race, a royal priesthood…a people for God's own possession."*

I made it to Knoxville just fine, but—wouldn't you know it—my luggage didn't. At seven the next morning, my luggage still had not arrived, and I am at the age at which I'd rather have my makeup than fresh clothes. You can shower-steam your clothes. All I had in the way of makeup was a powder compact, lipstick, and the pencil by the phone pad. (Yes, I did use it on my eyebrows!) I was to be on TV that morning. I promise you that I got on my knees, letting God remind me of my purpose and asking Him to shine through the natural me. As I dumped all the facts on my husband late that night, bewailing the circumstances, he said, "Oh honey! Those people didn't know but what you always have the natural look!" Just the word I needed! He was correct.

The next morning, a young mother with a small daughter picked me up to go to the mission meeting. The mother said to the daughter, "Honey, say hello to the missionary." Silence…as the pretty little girl looked me over. "Please say hello to the missionary. She is going to speak to our mission group this morning." More silence. I thought perhaps I should speak first. As I turned to speak to the little girl, she said, "Well, she looks a lot like a mommy to me!" Our world needs mommy missionaries, doctors, lawyers, teachers, beauticians, CEOs, librarians, and priests…priesting our circle of influence!

How can we live intentionally in the splashing mode? Well, I can't wait to share with you the eight patterns drawn from John's Gospel chapter four, which detail for us a simple and natural way to *splash the living water on those in our circles of influence.*

Pattern 1: Going Out of Your Way on Your Way

John 4:3–4, says, "[Jesus] *left Judea and went away again into Galilee. And He had to pass through Samaria.*" Jesus and His disciples had been spending time in Judea. When Jesus knew that the Pharisees were saying that He was baptizing more disciples than John, He left Judea and departed again to Galilee. This meant He chose to go out of His way—to get back to Galilee.

I believe Jesus made an intentional decision that day to go out of His way. I'm struck with the idea that you and I can do the same thing. While I am on my way to the grocery store, I can go out of my way to *splash* someone while I'm shopping. While I'm at the beauty shop, I can go out of my way to *splash* someone while I'm there. As kingdom citizens, we are on kingdom business every day in every way. A subject serves the king, not just part time, but all the time. When Jesus came to earth, He ushered in the kingdom of God. We live as subjects on the King's business. My life as a Christian is not just about a heavenly home. It is about living daily as a kingdom subject. Imagine living with such intentions that everything we do has eternal significance!

I know a pastor's wife who intentionally parks her car in the farthest corner of the grocery store parking lot, so she can *splash the living water* on the boy who takes her groceries to her car. She makes an intentional decision to share Christ. When I heard the story, I thought, "I can do that."

Going to the grocery store is not my favorite event of the week, but with new energy, I began to look for creative ways I could share Christ and *splash the living water*. I don't know about you, but the longest line at the grocery store always seems to find me. It just reaches out and grabs me—and there I stand, waiting for someone to get the discount coupons in order or to write a check. Shortly after my decision to splash more, I found myself facing a long-line situation and was getting frustrated when I remembered that I had planned to try to *splash the living water* in the grocery store that day. Evaluating my options, I found a young mother attempting to check out. She had a child in the child's seat of the shopping cart, another one in the front of the cart, and a third one being carried in her tummy basket. This grocery store—as most do—had all the gum and candy bars displayed right beside the checkout counter. What a menace that is to the young mother who is already at her wit's end. I saw my opportunity. As the children began to grab at the shelves, I came up behind and began talking to them...in my Nana voice. Almost any child will laugh when you play peek-a-boo with them or pretend to tickle them. I kept the children entertained as the young mother finished checking out.

When finished, she looked at me and expressed her thanks. I said, "My daughter has three little girls, and she is tired all the time. I know because when I visit, they tire me out, too. I'll do for you what I do for my daughter:

I'll pray for you today—that God will put His strength in your arms and His love in your heart, so you can be the mother that you want to be." She thanked me again as she walked away while the little ones and I waved to each other.

The next part of the story I am making up—but stay with me. If this young mother is typical, when her husband got home from work that night, she said to him, "You won't believe what happened to me at the grocery today. This gray-headed lady played with the children while I checked out the groceries, and then she told me she would pray for me today. How about that?"

What I am trusting to be true in regard to this grocery store encounter is that other Christians out there also include this young mother in their *circle of concern* and are obedient to *splash the living water* her way. I believe with all my heart that a great tool for sharing Christ is common courtesy. Try it. It seems we've lost this simple kindness, so people are surprised when they experience it. The husband may or may not have been impressed with her story, but the Holy Spirit was pleased.

What I am trusting about the Holy Spirit is something like this: on Tuesday of the next week, this tired young mother dragged herself to the PTA meeting and happened to sit next to a *splashing* Christian, who gave her another bit of encouragement. Two weeks later, she was in the doctor's office and picked up *Christian Parenting* magazine and found an article related to the very problem her six-year old was experiencing, and she found herself remembering the words of that grandmother in the grocery store—even though she may not understand the reason why. The nurse called, and she and the child entered the doctor's office. She then encountered a *splashing* nurse, who inquired about the reason for the visit. Being a woman, and a Christian who *goes out of her way on her way,* the nurse offered the mother words of encouragement and hope, even perhaps recalling when her child was in that stage of growth. Women, you can *splash the living water* like this all the time! It's a woman thing.

Let's continue with this thought pattern. The young mother was thirsty for this welcome information and wondered to herself why she was drawn to this nurse whose kind voice shared information exactly like the article she just read in the waiting room. What the unsuspecting mother didn't know was that God's precious Holy Spirit was at work managing the circumstances—drawing her to Himself.

Don't you want to live in the expectancy of what the Spirit chooses to do through your obedience as you go out of your way...on your way...*splashing the living water?* A citizen of God's kingdom is like a river about to spill over its banks...simply *splashing the living water.*

Pattern 2: Crossing Barriers with the Gospel

Jesus went to the city of Samaria called Sychar, which was near Jacob's well. Jesus was weary from His journey, so He sat down by the well. It was the noon hour. The disciples had gone into town to get Jesus something to eat. A Samaritan woman came to the well to draw her water for the day. Jesus asked her to give Him a drink.

It is difficult for us to grasp the significance of this encounter. She was a Samaritan, and He was a Jew. Generally, these two groups hated each other. Jews would cross the street, not wanting to be caught even in the shadow of a Samaritan. Samaritans were considered to be half-breed...unclean...less than...or whatever degrading words Jews could think to apply to them. So why would Jesus speak first? Also, Jesus was a rabbi. According to custom, only men had the privilege of learning from the rabbi. What a rebel this rabbi was. He came to call sinners—not the righteous—to repentance (see Luke 5:32). He was the Messiah; she was a sinner.

Jesus crossed every barrier possible to reach this woman: gender, racial, cultural, and sacred. Breaking tradition in any of these ways would have been formidable in that day. Jesus, offering living water, not only splashed the woman, but His good news met the thirst in her life as nothing ever had. He called it living water, a well of water—springing up, gushing out, forever thirst-quenching, life-giving water!

What are your barriers to sharing the living water today? When I ask this question in seminars, the two most common answers are always *fear* and *rejection.* Some other barriers might be *time, energy, education, social status,* or *attitude.* Perhaps other barriers exist. Remember 2 Timothy 1:7: *"For God has not given us a spirit of fear, but of power and of love and of a sound mind"* (NKJV). Since *"God has not given us a spirit of fear,"* from where do you suppose the fear comes?

Of course, it comes from the evil one...Satan. If he can use your fear of being rejected to keep you from obedience in sharing Christ, he will do so. He wins when you let your fear be a barrier. I know. I'm reserved, and for a long time, I listened to his voice telling me not to say anything about Christ because I was too shy. I believe that one of the great barriers to witnessing is just plain *disobedience,* which sometimes means just listening to the wrong voice.

We fear rejection, but we also fear failure. I define *lifestyle witnessing* as sharing Jesus Christ in the power of the Holy Spirit and leaving the results to God. I'm convinced that many Christians do not share Christ because they think they fail if they do not lead someone to Christ. You fail only if you fail to share!

Do you remember the encounter Jesus had with the rich young ruler in Luke 18? Jesus shared the truth and an invitation, but the man refused to accept the truth. Jesus just continued instructing and sharing with others, knowing He had been obedient to God. The rich young ruler walked away—very rich, but very sad. Think about this. If you share your faith story with someone and they reject your story, they are not rejecting you—they are rejecting Him. Don't take it personally.

In light of the gospel, we have been called to die for our faith. Yet we let fear of rejection keep us from even telling our faith story. When we understand the work of the Holy Spirit as we examined in a previous chapter, we know it is not our work to lead someone to Christ; it is, however, our task to be a vessel through which the Holy

Spirit can work. He, the Holy Spirit, does the drawing to Christ. This reality became a freeing truth for my life when I recognized that God is the power at work through me. I am not in this alone. As my friend Thelma Bagby used to say: "God and me. That's enough!"

I believe another one of the greatest barriers to *splashing the living water* in today's culture is the church. When I first began teaching a seminar on lifestyle witnessing, I asked the audience to write down the names of people in their lives who did not know Christ. I watched, and no pencils were moving. Then I said, hoping to make them more comfortable: "Just describe the person. Do they look like a mail carrier?" Still no pencils moved. It made me realize a huge truth: Christians make most, if not all, of their friends inside the church, and they know few lost people. I then asked the audience, "Where have you been in the last 48 hours?" The women were able to respond to that question:

- Beauty shop
- Grocery store
- Hospital
- School
- Church

I then asked, "Were there any lost people there?" They all nodded their heads. I then asked, "Were there any Christians there?" I could see the truth dawn on them. Everywhere they go, they are on a mission field, and they are the missionaries—the sent ones, with the good news.

It is my observation that we make our friends in the church with those who look like us, dress like us, act like us, and go to the same schools and clubs as we do. How convenient. How comfortable. How unlike Christ! *The church can be a barrier.* Some churches offer Bible study, worship, meals, exercise, and recreation—making it unnecessary for Christians to do anything outside their own church. We even build huge sports complexes and fields and organize teams within the church and post signs: MEMBERS ONLY. How ludicrous!

Back to our story. The disciples returned with food for the Teacher. The disciples were much like us; they did not recognize the reality and truth right in front of their eyes. The Teacher modeled the great commission, and the Word says, *"And at this point His disciples came, and they marveled that He talked with a woman; yet no one said, 'What do You seek?' or, 'Why are You talking with her?'"* (John 4:27). Consider this thought: **Who marvels at your life because of those to whom you choose to speak?**

I once watched as the following story unfolded. A group of high school girls from Georgia belonged to a missions organization called Acteens®. They told their missions leader they wished to really do something with the group that would make a difference in their lives and in the community. Looking around the neighborhood for a project, the leader discovered a home for unwed mothers very near their church, and the Acteens decided to go for it. The group introduced themselves to the management and offered help. The management representative said: "Just offer friendship. These girls are just like you—except they are pregnant." Those teenage Acteen girls discovered other teenage girls, 14, 15, and 17, who were pregnant and feeling alone.

The Acteens began going to the home one afternoon per week after school—just offering friendship. The girls from the home asked if they could come to the Acteens meeting at the church. "Sure," they said. "Why not!" Sometime later, the girls from the home decided to come to the Wednesday youth Bible study. The Acteens checked it out with the youth group. Again, they were given the go-ahead. They told the other youth, "When we bring our friends, don't dare look at them." Can't you just see that youth group—trying to *not* look at the pregnant girls as they came to the Bible study? You have to love young people. They can be so accepting.

The girls then began coming to Sunday morning worship. What a sight it was! The youth always sat in the center—right down front—in the worship service. Sprinkled among the church youth were these precious pregnant teens. Wow! The church looked like the church—a shelter for recovering sinners! I was very proud of our church.

It was at the Bible study that the youth minister announced the upcoming overnight lock-in. The Acteens took on babysitting and work projects in order to earn extra money so they could pay the way for their new friends to attend the lock-in. Talk about crossing barriers with the gospel—this was it!

During the weekend, Tonya—who had been kicked out of her home at age 14, had lived on the streets, was involved in drugs, alcohol, and sex—learned of God's amazing love through the Bible study and the example of her new friends. She prayed to receive Jesus as her Savior. I happened to be in service the Sunday morning she was baptized. I was sitting with my then-college-age son, David. As Tonya came up from the baptismal waters, she, in almost a shout, said, "Yes, yes!" The body of Christ in our church broke into applause. I leaned over to my son and said, "The only difference between Tonya and me is that her sin shows and mine doesn't always show." What a glorious day for Tonya and for the Acteens, who really wanted to do something positive for the kingdom—and they crossed barriers to do it. When Jesus crossed the barriers at the well that day, an entire city was exposed to the truth, and many came to know Him as Savior.

Pattern 3: Sharing the Gift You Have Within

Let's return to the conversation between the Samaritan woman and Jesus in verse 10: *"Jesus answered and said to her, 'If you knew the gift of God, and who it is who says to you, "Give Me a drink," you would have asked Him, and He would have given you living water'"* (John 4:10).

What truth He declared to her! He was speaking of Himself, God's gift of salvation. If you know Jesus as your personal Savior, then you have the gift of God within you. That is the gift we are to splash on others. This gift of God within you is not about your spiritual gifts, abilities, or talents, though God uses those. The gift of God within you is His gift of salvation. Then it would be out of that relationship that you would *splash the living water.* The gift of God is your story of how you came to know and abide in this personal relationship.

From the day that I received Christ as a seven-year-old child until this day, I have had the gift of God within me. I'm sure you have heard the old song, "I'll Tell the World That I'm A Christian." I wanted to tell everyone that I belonged to God's family forever. Why is it we soon get away from that childlike first love of sharing about Christ? I was a good witness until my teen years; then I let being a teenager keep me from sharing my faith. My thinking was, *Let them see Christ in me, and when they see the difference, they will ask me about it.* The only problem with that thinking is this: it does not work. No one has ever asked me about my relationship to God without me first initiating the opportunity in some way. I had to learn that sharing my faith is not either/or. It is both/and. It is sometimes getting to minister but not getting to share Christ; other times, it is sharing Christ but not getting to minister. The bottom line is **obedience.** If you can establish obedience as a pattern in your life, you will see many opportunities to speak and minister in His name.

Pattern 4: Turning a Conversation

Jesus was a master in turning a conversation from earthly issues to heavenly issues. In the John 4:19–24 narrative, Jesus and the Samaritan woman had a religious conversation. She knew the history of Jacob's well. She knew about temple worship in Jerusalem. Jesus, after telling her the most important words of her life—the truth of the **living water**—then told her a very significant fact about true worship.

> *Jesus said to her, "Woman, believe Me, an hour is coming when neither in this mountain nor in Jerusalem will you worship the Father. You worship what you do not know; we worship what we know, for salvation is from the Jews. But an hour is coming, and now is, when the true worshipers will worship the Father in spirit and truth; for such people the Father seeks to be His worshipers. God is spirit, and those who worship Him must worship in spirit and truth."*
>
> —John 4:21–24

After Jesus presented this short lesson on worship, the woman at the well replied, *"I know that Messiah is coming (He who is called Christ); when that One comes, He will declare all things to us"* (John 4:25). I think Jesus smiled in His heart, and said to her, *"I who speak to you am He"* (John 4:26). Fall down slack jawed! Cover your mouth with both hands! Did you really hear what He said? In the original language, it reads, *"The one who speaks to you is I AM."* In Exodus 3:14, we are introduced to I AM: *"God said to Moses, 'I AM WHO I AM'; and He said, 'Thus you shall say to the sons of Israel, "I AM has sent me to you.""'* The conversation between Jesus and the Samaritan woman turned from religious information to eternal truth—I AM!

You, too, can learn, with the Holy Spirit's help, to turn a conversation from religious information to eternal truth. Most of us are good with religious conversation. We talk about our church or Bible study. We talk about our denomination or about a certain speaker. That is just *religious talk.* That is *not* splashing the living water. *Splashing the living water is making someone thirsty for the living water—*then *offering the cup* of living water that Jesus so freely gives.

Many people in our world are comfortable having a conversation about religion or about God. It is quite a different thing to converse about Jesus and His saving power. Most people know something about God, but the key issue is this: Do they know about God's work through His Son on the cross?

If you are at the place where you can only have religious conversations, don't be discouraged. That is a beginning. You can then ask God to help you learn to turn a conversation, to be able to give a word of testimony, to lift up the name of Jesus, and to move the conversation to eternal truth. In telling someone about your weekly Bible study, turn the conversation by sharing why it is important in your life to go to Bible study—to seek to learn eternal truths by which to live. This subtle turn may lead to the opportunity for you to ask this person to join you in Bible study.

At 5:30 one morning, a van arrived to take me to the airport in Oklahoma City. As the gentleman took my luggage and put it in the van, he asked me on what airline would I be traveling. I told him Delta. He then said, "Well, you must be going to Atlanta." I guess he had the early morning run and knew all the schedules.

"Yes, I am—and you know what they say about Atlanta!"

"No. What do they say?" He responded.

"They say if you're going to heaven, you've got to go through Atlanta. Just between you and me, that's not really what they say. They say if you're going to [pointing down], you must go through Atlanta."

The gentleman replied quickly, "You know, lady, there's only one way to heaven—and that is through the cross of Jesus Christ." I had tried to turn our conversation to the truth, but he beat me to the punch. Since we were kin in Christ, I moved up to the front seat, and we shared Christ all the way to the airport. He took my luggage all the way to the Delta counter. I gave him a good tip. He gave me a big hug. God smiled as an older gentleman and a grandmother hugged in Christ that morning. My brother in Christ knew how to turn a conversation to lift up the Savior!

Another time I was at the airport, I chose to ride the cart from gate 3 to gate 33—which is a long way at the Dallas International Airport! At one of the stops, a priest got on the cart and sat down by me. He asked cheerfully, "Is Dallas your home?"

I was startled and tried my best to remember where I lived at the moment. You might say I was having a senior moment. Bob and I had just moved. "No," I finally stumbled.

"It's not mine either," he said. "Mine is Cloud 22."

"If yours is 22, then mine is 23!"

He laughed with me, and gave me the high five! "Praise God. Then you know Jesus!"

I said I did. We *splashed the living water* all over the cart that day as we talked about our relationship to Jesus.

My suspicion is that perhaps this priest rides the cart all day—every day—just splashing folks with the same question and hoping for the same answer. I smile, thinking about the refreshment he was to my life. Ask God to teach you to learn to turn the conversation and to bring glory to the Father.

Pattern 5: Confronting the Sin

After Jesus shared with the Samaritan woman that He could give her life-giving water like a well, springing up to eternal life, and she asked Him to give it to her, the conversation took another turn.

> Jesus...said to her, "Everyone who drinks of this water will thirst again; but whoever drinks of the water that I will give him shall never thirst; but the water that I will give him will become in him a well of water springing up to eternal life."
>
> The woman said to Him, "Sir, give me this water, so I will not be thirsty nor come all the way here to draw."

> *He said to her, "Go, call your husband
> and come here."*
>
> —John 4:13–16

Do you see that subtle turn in conversation? Jesus said to her, *"Go, call your husband and come here."* What did Jesus know that led Him to ask about her husband after she asked for the living water? He knew her thirst. I picture this woman, caught once again by her lifestyle, hanging her head and quietly answering, "I have... I have no husband."

Just imagine with me what might have happened. Jesus may have reached toward her, lifted her chin so their eyes could meet, and tenderly said, "I know, daughter. You have bravely told the truth. Let's talk about your husbands. Let's talk about your thirst."

Surprised at what Jesus knew about her, the woman responded to Him, *"Sir, I perceive that You are a prophet"* (John 4:19).

Jesus, in the part of the story just discussed, modeled for us another pattern—confronting the sin. I believe it was at the moment that Jesus confronted the woman with her sin by asking her to get her husband that she knew in her heart He was the Messiah. I believe that when Jesus looked into her eyes, He saw her sinful heart. She must have been awakened to her sin as He detailed so vividly her background.

Jesus was so relational. Jesus first drew this woman to the living water He had to offer, then confronted her with her sin. As you move about in your circles of concern, you will find that as relationships develop, some situations develop in which you, like Jesus, must confront the person with the cost of sin and the eternal separation that results from sin. We cannot tell a person all about Jesus and never tell them that *"the wages of sin is death, but the free gift of God is eternal life in Christ Jesus our Lord"* (Romans 6:23).

Dr. Roy Fish, a Southwestern Baptist Theological Seminary professor, provided the tool I use for confronting the sin. He suggests that you say, "Has anyone ever told you who Jesus is, or would you say you are in the process of discovering who He is?" If they respond by saying they are in the process, ask them to share. Very often in examining that process, a person is led to confront their sin. That opens the door for you to share your journey. I feel very comfortable using the question suggested by Dr. Fish and find it works for my personality. This whole concept of splashing the living water is individualized by your personality, your spiritual gifts, and your communication style all under obedience to the Heavenly Father. He does not ask me to share like Billy Graham. I couldn't. I'm Esther Burroughs. The same is true for you: You are who you are.

At times, you will find yourself doing what you thought you could not do. When I first began to travel, my friend Ruth Ward heard me in a teaching session tell that I was shy and that it was hard for me to go door to door to present the claims of Christ. Being an author about personality types, she came to me privately and said, "You are not shy; you are reserved. There is a difference. You can draw a reserved person into a conversation by finding out an interest. That will help them open up." This was such good news to me. I had used my shyness to keep from sharing Christ. I realized that as a reserved person, I usually let the other person take the lead in a conversation; that feels comfortable to me and is easier for me than jumping right in to share my relationship to Christ. As a reserved person, if you ask me questions about things I'm interested in, I will open up and talk. And talking provides the opportunity to gently turn conversation.

Ruth continued, "By the way, as you travel and share Christ on the airplane, that is just like going door to door!" I now recognize that the airlines are part of my neighborhood and office.

Let me illustrate this pattern by sharing events from a recent trip. Being obedient to the Spirit's leading and minding my own business...tray table up...Bible open and notebook in hand...ready to study and write, I studied while waiting for the plane to take off. A man sat down in the seat next to me. He reached out and grabbed my arm and said, "Hey babe! How ya doing?" Well, I'll tell you that my body stiffened! No one calls me Babe but *my* Babe. My voice and body language gave a brief and cool greeting, and I turned back to my work. As he settled into his seat, he touched my arm again, babbling on about the weather. I thought to myself that maybe I should show him my granddaughter photos. Then he would leave me alone. I acted very busy with my notebook, hoping he would leave me alone. He continued to chat as he eyed my Bible.

"How long you been religious?"

Still acting cool, I said, "I grew up in a minister's family and came to know about God's love as a child."

"Well, how about that!" He laughed. "I just bet you go to church all the time and really believe in all that stuff."

By then, I was thinking, *He is either thirsty for the living water, or he is making fun of me, so maybe I need an attitude adjustment.*

As soon as the plane leveled off, the flight attendants began to serve the meal. Putting my Bible in my lap, I accepted the meal, but he turned down the meal, saying, "Oh no, I have big plans for the evening!"

Prior to eating, I bowed my head as I usually do and said a blessing for my meal. As I lifted my head, he said quietly, "Oh, you're very religious!"

Looking at him for the first time, I replied, "It is a habit I learned in my childhood, and I can't imagine not thanking God for everything He gives, and besides I asked for a safe journey home."

His next action caught me completely off guard. He leaned over and took my Bible off my lap! I raised my eyebrows, and thought about getting off the plane somehow. But when I caught my breath, he was silently thumbing through the pages of my Bible, seemingly looking for a Scripture.

At that moment, the Holy Spirit whispered to me, "Help him." I don't know if you talk back to the Spirit, but I do, and I explained to the Spirit that this man was the same man who was touching me and calling me Babe. Again, I heard, "Help him." *No, Father, not this man....* But in my arguing with the Spirit, I heard myself say, "Bill" (I'd learned his name by this time), "may I help you?" He pulled a scrap piece of paper from his pocket, and said, "I've been looking for a Bible for six months."

What a flowing river event for me—there I was, a *living* Bible (a *living letter,* Paul says), with a *physical* Bible available at God's disposal.

Bill showed me the slip of paper and handed me my Bible. I noted the Scripture and looked it up for him. Being a woman, I read it to myself and noted it spoke about forgiveness; then I passed the Bible back to him and showed him the verse. He read in silence, but could not keep back his tears.

As he began to weep, he said through his tears, "I'm having an affair."

Caught off guard again, I tried to not show my shock and to make a smile happen. At the same time, I was trying to keep from swallowing my tongue! In fast-forward, I was thinking: *What do I say now? Are you having a good time? How is it going? Oh my! Does your wife know?* No need for worry...he spoke first.

"My daughter is a Christian like you, and she wrote my wife a letter. I read it. My daughter asked my wife to forgive me and to let us start over."

He never even took a breath. He fast-forwarded the story.

"But I don't want to stop the affair, and I don't want to lose my family. I'm embarrassed to tell you that my wife is like you. She loves God and God's Word. She's a Christian, just like you, and I've ruined her life. Do you think she could ever forgive me?"

He really did not mean for me to answer. He kept on talking. "My children hate me. I'm about to destroy my life. I'm so ashamed. I'm embarrassed to tell you I am a Christian, too—just like you—and I know I'm wrong."

Wow! At this point, I knew how to answer. "Bill, do you know why you are crying? You have broken God's law. When you break God's law, it breaks God's heart. His desire is that we live in fellowship with Him, but when we sin, we break that fellowship. It feels like hiding from His holiness."

"I know," he whispered.

I was amazed at myself—talking with passion to this man whom I had all but ignored and being bold enough to talk about his sin! That is how the Spirit leads us—even when we do not want to be led.

I tried to explain to Bill that his daughter was trying to give her mother the same message. On our journey through life, we will all sin. But God's forgiveness at the cross is forever...past, present, and future. I told Bill that he needed to repent of his sin, confess it to God, confess to his family, and ask for their forgiveness. I assured him that God's love was so powerful that this sin could be forgiven and even forgotten, and that God was capable of putting his marriage back together in such a way that God would receive glory!

As he cried, I felt so helpless and wished for a godly man to be sitting close by—someone with great words of wisdom for him. As the plane was landing, I reached into my purse to get a tract to give to him to reinforce what I had shared with him. As I pulled it out, my hands happened to open it to the page that illustrated repentance and forgiveness. (Well, perhaps it wasn't *my* hand that actually opened to that page.) I said, "Bill, here it is. *Repent* means to turn away, walk away from the sin, accept God's forgiveness, and start over." He thanked me as we got off the plane together, and as I walked away, he called out, "Esther! Pray for me!" I did and I continue to do so.

The next morning in staff meeting as the group shared, I told them the story that you have just read and said, "If only one of you guys had been sitting beside Bill, it would have made a difference." A friend in the group quietly said, "He probably would not have told a man what he told you...because you are a woman." Yes! God chooses to work through women as He calls us into relationship with Himself, and He wants to minister in and through our relationships. Bill was a *person X* in my circle of influence, but he was also in his daughter's and wife's inner circles. God's Holy Spirit is always working to draw persons to Jesus Christ. I want to live in the expectation of God's Spirit working through my obedience, allowing daily interruptions to become divine encounters.

Be open to God choosing to use you in carefully and lovingly confronting others with the good news of forgiveness and new life.

Pattern 6: Satisfying the Hungry and Thirsty with Living Water

I imagine the conversation between Jesus and the Samaritan woman took quite some time, considering the number of issues covered in the conversation plus the fact that Jesus was not in a hurry. He was just waiting around, since His disciples had gone to town for food.

When the disciples returned from town, they marveled that Jesus *"had been speaking with a woman; yet no one said, 'What do You seek?' or, 'Why do You speak with her?'"* (John 4:27). The disciples were mostly concerned with meeting Jesus's physical needs with the food they had brought back. They kept insisting, *"Rabbi, eat"* (John 4:31).

Jesus said to them, *"I have food to eat that you do not know about"* (John 4:32).

Now, that statement confused the disciples; they were questioning one another, *"No one brought Him* [a burger and fries] *to eat, did he?"* (John 4:33). You have to laugh. They thought they were in charge of His eating. They were concerned that someone else had brought food to the Teacher before they had gotten back from town. Listen to His answer; it is profound for us to hear in today's overscheduled culture of micromanagers, always on top and in control of the situation!

> *Jesus said to them, "My food is to do the will of Him who sent Me and to accomplish His work."*
>
> —John 4:34

Translated literally, Jesus said, "I have just eaten of God." No wonder He walks through the gospel of John calling Himself the Bread of life. *"Jesus said to them, 'I am the bread of life; he who comes to Me will not hunger, and he who believes in Me will never thirst'"* (John 4:35). The Bread of life shared the living water with the woman—feeding her soul and filling His. He was so full spiritually that He was not hungry physically. Don't be surprised. That is exactly what you and I feel when we have a chance to share the living water with someone.

"So the woman left her waterpot, and went into the city and said to the men, 'Come, see a man who told me all the things that I have done; this is not the Christ, is it?'" (John 4:28–29). Do you suppose she forgot the water pot in the excitement of the disciples' return, or because she had such good news to share, or having received the whole **well of living water**, she no longer needed a water pot? Perhaps all three. Just imagine the stir this created in town:

- The thoughts of the men who knew her so intimately
- The astonishment of the women who kept their distance
- The joy she displayed in her perception about the Messiah
- Her delight in introducing her village to Jesus.

"From that city many of the Samaritans believed in Him because of the word of the woman who testified, 'He told me all the things that I have done'" (John 4:39). The

living water replaced physical and spiritual hunger. The Word can do that for you and me...even today.

Consider this: When the disciples went into the village, they brought back only food. When the woman went into the village, she brought back the entire village. Look at it again: The disciples, who knew the Bread of life, went to town, but brought back only physical bread. The woman, having just met the Bread of life who gave her living water, carried that living water to town, and brought back the hungry and thirsty people, so they could receive living water for themselves as they personally encountered the Bread of life. Perhaps the meeting of Jesus and the Samaritan woman at the well was just a chance encounter, but I would say it was more likely *a divine encounter.* One Messiah. One Samaritan woman and one village **splashed by the living water**—forever changed because of one woman's thirst.

Some time ago after a storm, I flew up the east coast for a speaking engagement. I barely made my connection through the Atlanta airport, but I did make it to the event with no trouble. After speaking that night, I got to the hotel and unpacked my luggage. It was Valentine's Day weekend, so I was not surprised to find a card hidden in my luggage. I smiled as I read what my husband had written: "When you get home this weekend, we'll party... *(dot, dot, dot).*" Well, I thought about those *dots* all weekend—and couldn't wait to get home.

After teaching the next morning, I made my way to the Harrisburg, Pennsylvania, airport in seven inches of snow, not the least concerned about my flight. After all, they know about snow in the North. I had laid my ticket down on the counter, waiting for the attendant to check my bag, when he said, "Mrs. Burroughs, this flight is canceled."

"It can't be," I protested.

"Well, it is! See that sign?"

"You don't understand! I'm on my way home to dot, dot, dot!"

He looked at me, showing by his expression that he did not understand—and I was not about to explain.

"When is the next flight?"

"Four hours from now," was the reply. Then he said, "By the way, you have a ticket from Harrisburg to Atlanta—but not one from Atlanta to West Palm Beach."

This was too much bad news for a little gal who had just had her valentine party canceled. After searching my purse, the tears began to flow.

He said, "Let me look this up." As he did, I am sure he saw that I was a platinum-level frequent flyer. He smiled and said, "Let me fix that ticket for you." Believe me, this does not happen in today's market.

I cried some more. Tears work for me! Four hours to wait...getting home past midnight...small plastic chairs in the waiting area...coffee from a machine—it was not looking good. I called home, and received a warm greeting.

"Hey Babe! Glad to hear from you. How ya doing?"

"Not good," I teared.

"What's the matter?"

"Tell me I love what God's called me to do."

"You *do* love what you are doing! Why?"

"My plane has been delayed, and I won't get home until midnight!"

"No problem," he laughed. "We'll just party at midnight!"

That's a problem; you see, *I don't party at midnight!* I might party at 9:30 or maybe 10:00…but not midnight! After I received his encouragement, we said good-bye.

Boarding the crowded plane four hours later, I took my seat by a young couple. Settling in, I asked the young woman, Patricia by name, if she lived in Harrisburg. Patricia grew up in the area, but now lived in West Palm Beach and was back home for her grandfather's funeral. My mother's heart was immediately touched, and I expressed my sadness for her. She began telling me about being raised by her grandmother. I listened. She told me how she had, as a small child, learned Bible verses and songs from her grandmother and had gone to church all her life. She said of her grandmother, "She taught me that Jesus loved me. She led me to love Jesus."

"What a great faith heritage you have," I said. I shared a little about my childhood home, and we both acknowledged our faith in Christ. Then she whispered, pointing to her husband, "But he doesn't." (Isn't that just like a woman? We tell everything!) We talked a long time about her grandparents. She needed a listening heart and a strong shoulder on which to lean. I asked her what church they attended in West Palm Beach. She told me they were newlyweds and hadn't started church yet. Then I gave her my grandmotherly advice, sharing how important the body of Christ is to newlyweds as they establish their marriage.

As Patricia and I talked about the church, her young husband, Michael, leaned over in front of her and said, "That man yesterday at the funeral...the ah...pastor... yes, the pastor...talked about a 'shepherd' leading us."

I said, "Did he talk about *'the Lord is my shepherd, I shall not want? He makes me to lie down in green pastures, He leads me...'*"

"Yes," he interrupted! "That shepherd! Do you know the shepherd?"

All of a sudden I knew why my flight had been canceled. I told him about the Great Shepherd of Psalm 23, and how, as a small girl, I had understood God's love for me. I told him how I had learned that this Great Shepherd wanted to be *my shepherd* and friend through the rest of my life.

Then Mike asked me a question that stopped my heart. "If you've never been in a church in all your life, how do you get in one?"

I smiled, knowing I couldn't wait to tell my dot, dot, dot guy about this young man. I told Mike, who by now was leaning across his wife and quietly listening to my words, the story of the shepherd who had 99 sheep in the pen but one sheep was missing. The shepherd went looking for that one lost sheep. "It is the Shepherd's work to look after His sheep and guide them," I said, referring to our Great Shepherd. "He is the kind of shepherd that knows every sheep by name. Mike, all you have to do to get to know this Shepherd is to confess your lostness and accept His love for you, which will admit you into the fold of the Shepherd's family forever."

His eyes filled with tears as he listened. Patricia added her voice as she cried about her grandfather, who she knew had gone home to the Good Shepherd. The presence of the Holy Spirit was so real in our conversation. Mike agreed he would think about the Shepherd's invitation. As we began to exit the plane, they both thanked me and promised they would find a church. I gave them the name of a church near them because I knew the pastor as a friend and said I would call him and tell him this story.

I got off the plane just *dancing*. I know that's not Baptist...or Nazarene...but it is very biblical. King David, the shepherd king, who loved the Good Shepherd, danced before the Lord. My husband was there to meet me with a bouquet of flowers. I'm sure he was expecting me to be dragging. Was he ever surprised! I bounded over to him and hugged him furiously! "What happened to you?" he asked.

"Let me introduce you to Patricia and Mike."

Bob smiled knowingly.

Often, I find myself submitting in obedience to circumstances beyond my control and wondering why—knowing I will be shown the reason. How wonderful it is that God continues to be as patient with us as with the disciples. All they were thinking about was physical food; all I was thinking about was getting to West Palm Beach on time for...dot, dot, dot. *Kingdom living is rich.* I miss it so often when I plow ahead with my own agenda, thinking on-time flights are what matter, but being surprised by the blessing of a late flight with funeral attenders who had a need for the Shepherd. I'm glad God allowed me to have the encounter, because it was encouragement and spiritual food to my own heart.

Pattern 7: Seeing the Fields with Compassion

> *Do you not say, "There are yet four months,*
> *and then comes the harvest"? Behold, I say to*
> *you, lift up your eyes and look on the fields,*
> *that they are white for harvest.*

—John 4:35

Jesus—always the Teacher—often used word pictures to help the disciples see.

Having grown up with farming grandparents, I can see, in my mind's eye, the white tip wheat waving in the prairie winds. I was familiar with the harvest machinery that enabled Granddad to do his work. Some field was always in a state ready for harvest—which made for long hours in those fields season after season.

In my childhood Sunday school class, pictures on the wall defined biblical characters in long, flowing, white or ecru robes, tied with bright-colored sashes. My mental picture of these characters makes it easy for me to see the point of Jesus's example. Imagine with me: The Samaritan woman is at the front of the crowd. The villagers, dressed in flowing garments, follow her back to the well. She encourages, "Come on! See for yourself! This is the Messiah!" All the way to the well, she repeats her story over and over. "Hurry! We are almost there. See, that's Him—the one sitting by the well!" For real, many of the Samaritans believed in Him that day because of the woman who testified.

Now fast-forward to the well.

Jesus is still teaching His disciples. I imagine that He might even clap His hands together to indicate, Listen up, guys! Get this! *"Lift up your eyes and look on the fields."* Pointing to the crowd—the white-unto-harvest field coming toward Him—He makes the point again, "Look at the fields!" as He motions toward the crowd coming. "They are ready to harvest!"

When Jesus said, *"Look on the fields,…they are white for harvest,"* I think He meant the people—the people-harvest of the Samaritan village. These villagers invited Jesus to stay two days, and many more came to know Him through direct contact with Him—the provider of living water. They said, *"We have heard for ourselves and know that this One is indeed the Savior of the world"* (John 4:42).

The heart of Jesus was compassionate for the people to know His Father. I long to develop *eyes for the harvest —seeing the fields with a heart of compassion.*

I heard an evangelist share the following story. A man with a heart for the harvest felt compassion for an upper-class neighborhood. After much prayer, he began to visit in that community. At the first place he visited, a woman came to the door. The visitor tried to tell her about Jesus. Slamming the door in his face, she yelled that she had no interest at all in Jesus! Not wanting to give up too easily, the visitor sat down on the steps and began to sing,

> *Alas and did my Savior bleed,*
>   *and did my Sov'reign die?*
> *Would He devote that sacred Head*
>   *for sinners such as I?*
> *But drops of grief can ne'er repay*
>   *the debt of love I owe;*
> *Here, Lord, I give [my life] away,*
>   *'Tis all that I can do.*
> *At the cross, at the cross*
>   *where I first saw the light,*
> *and the burden of my heart rolled away...*

Little did he know that the woman listened to his song behind a drawn curtain. All day long, she struggled. When her husband returned home, he found her in tears. She told him what had happened. He said, "Forget it. You made him leave. It's over."

"I can't forget it," she cried.

"What can't you forget?" he challenged her.

"It's the 'drops of grief' that I can't forget," she answered.

One man...*seeing the world with a heart of compassion*...making an eternal difference!

Pattern 8: Sowing and Reaping, Enlarging the Kingdom

There is more to see in the lesson Jesus was teaching His disciples at the well in Samaria. Let's look again at that teaching session: *"Already he who reaps is receiving wages and is gathering fruit for life eternal; so that he who sows and he who reaps may rejoice together"* (John 4:36).

The Teacher pointed out a wonderful truth at the well that day. I'm glad it is the last pattern for us to consider, because it has the power to free us to splash indiscriminately...free of guilt...free of concern about results. *Free!* ***Free! FREE!***

Jesus gave equal weight to ***sowing*** and ***reaping.*** Evangelical Christians tend to do just the opposite; they try to make reaping *the most important* part of the experience. Not Jesus. He states that the sower and the reaper rejoice together. That must mean they work together. What wonderful news! I can celebrate when the Spirit draws a person to Himself through me—and I see the result. And I can celebrate when the Spirit draws a person to Himself through me—but I see no results. I can celebrate whether I am the sower of the seed or the harvester in the field. Keep in mind: The harvest is not the end of the meeting or event...it is the ***end of the age.*** And He is the Harvester. We are His field hands. The field is His, and we work in joy together, knowing He will ultimately bring in the harvest.

What an affront it must be to Jesus when we refer to *my* Bible study group, *my* choir, or *my* mission project. Does He just cover His eyes and wonder if we will ever understand kingdom authority? The veil of the temple was rent one time! We do not have to protect it. We do not have to defend it through denominations, creeds, or worship structure. We are the stewards He has chosen to work in His field. We work with Him and for Him...not for ourselves or for our own personal ministry. This takes the *splashing results* right out of our hands and keeps them right in the Spirit's control, where they belong. More fun...guilt-free fun.

Perhaps too much importance has been placed on harvesting and the method of presentation, robbing the everyday believer of even trying to splash! How could we imagine that the Creator God—who designs us in His image, yet unique, particular, and holy—would ever expect all of us to splash in just the same way? Jesus Himself ministered in different ways in different circumstances. Being unique individuals, we each splash in a unique way. We should splash freely and trust the Holy Spirit to guide us when we are sowing and when we are reaping.

Live in the expectancy of the power of the Holy Spirit, working in each of us in every circumstance, to bring glory to Himself. I want that, don't you? He invites us to splash the living water as kingdom citizens, on kingdom business, with kingdom authority.

One of my favorite devotions in the book *My Utmost for His Highest* by Oswald Chambers is that for September 6. It is entitled, "Streams of Living Water," and references John 7:38.

A river touches places of which its source knows nothing, and Jesus says if we have received of His fullness, however small the visible measure of our lives, out of us will flow the rivers that will bless to the uttermost parts of the earth. We have nothing to do with the outflow— "This is the work of God that ye *believe....*" God rarely allows a soul to see how great a blessing he is.

A river is victoriously persistent; it overcomes all barriers. For a while, it goes steadily on its course, then it comes to an obstacle and for a while it is baulked, but it soon makes a pathway round the obstacle. Or a river will drop out of sight for miles, and presently emerge again broader and grander than ever. You can see God using some lives, but into your life an obstacle has come and you do not seem to be of any use. Keep paying attention to the Source, and God will either take you round the obstacle or remove it. The river of the Spirit of God overcomes all obstacles. Never get your eyes on the obstacle or on the difficulty. The obstacle is a matter of indifference to the river, which will flow steadily through you if you remember to keep right at the Source. Never allow anything to come between yourself and Jesus Christ, no emotion, or experience; nothing must keep you from the one great sovereign Source.

Think of the healing and far-flung rivers nursing themselves in our souls! God has been opening up marvelous truths to our minds, and at every point He has opened up is an indication of the wider power of the river He will flow through us. If you believe in Jesus, you will find that God has nourished in you mighty torrents of blessing for others.

—Oswald Chambers,
My Utmost for His Highest,
September 6

Our lives are to be channels through which the love of Jesus can flow—rivers of living water. Keeping the focus of our lives on Jesus Christ allows the continual flowing of God's power through us. In John 7:38, Jesus says, *"He who believes in Me...From his innermost being will flow rivers of living water."*

We can pray, "God, make me obedient...to drink in a stream of the living water and splash out the living water, so that others become thirsty, desiring to drink of the living water." The well is not an end in itself but becomes the source from which a river flows.

Do you remember my walking friend who finally came with Bible in hand to my home and said, "I want to know the peace you have"? The day that she came to my home and we talked, she recalled that as a child she loved Jesus, but this day was different. She really wanted a relationship with Him. I showed her John 3:16 and shared how my teacher had shown me as a child that the *"whosoever"* in that verse was a place I could put my name. I shared how I prayed, asking Jesus into my heart, and accepted His gift of eternal life. It was like the light dawned in her, and the questions about this new relationship poured out. It was fun to watch her thirst for

Him and be satisfied in the Word. Our walks became discipleship times. Yes, the struggles were still there, but now His love was there, also.

Let me share another encounter that occurred a year later on one of my flights back to Atlanta, where we lived at the time. My seat was by the window. The aisle seat was taken by a man who was already settled and thoroughly engrossed in a book, and the seat between ours was vacant. The man did not look up or speak as I passed by him to get to my seat.

Later as the meal was served, he placed the book in the seat between us. I glanced at the title; the book was *Codependent No More* by Melody Beattie. I casually said, "Good book you're reading!"

"You know this book?"

"I do."

"Well, I've just been home to visit family. I am getting things sorted out. What I really want is to be empowered."

"I know a little about that, also. I just wrote a book called *Empowered*."

"I'd like a copy, if you don't mind."

"I don't have it with me, but if you give me your card, I will send you a copy when I get home."

"Great. Where do you live?"

"Atlanta," I said.

"Me, too. Where in Atlanta?"

"I live in Lullwater Estates."

"This woman in my office lives there also, and she is empowered. All of a sudden, she brings our staff together and she prays over decisions."

"What work do you do?" I inquired.

"I'm a graphic artist."

"Really? What company?"

"Lewis, Clarke & Graham."

Hesitantly, I asked, "Do you know Stacy?"

"That's the woman I'm talking about!"

"She's my neighbor," I laughed.

"Then you must be Esther! She talks about you all the time."

Wow!

Safely home, I unlocked my front door and put down my luggage. The phone was ringing. It was my neighbor Stacy. "Bob just told me he met you on an airplane!"

"It's true."

"Wow," she said! "Now there are two of us talking to him about the Lord."

"Three," I reminded her. "Who but God could have arranged these circumstances?"

Women, delight in His love—lavished upon you. His love goes to any length to show His glory through you as you:

- *Go out of your way* to share on your way
- *Cross barriers* with the good news
- *Share the gift* you have within
- *Turn conversations* to the topic that matters
- *Confront sin* to initiate repentance
- *Guide others to the Satisfier* of their spiritual hunger and thirst

- **See the fields** with a heart of compassion
- **Reap the harvest**... through the power of the Holy Spirit!

My dear reader, choose to live in the expectancy of the Holy Spirit managing the circumstances of your life as you **splash the living water.**

Splashed and Splashing

1. What things about your life cannot be explained apart from the Holy Spirit?
2. Does your lifestyle make others thirsty to know the joy of the **living water?**
3. Would you consider living in such a way as to choose to deliberately **splash the living water?**
4. In your relationships with other people, is there an eternal impact because of your spreading of the **fragrance of Christ Jesus?**
5. Consider praying this prayer right now:
   "God, make me obedient in my walk to splash the living water until others develop a thirst and come to drink. Amen."

New Hope® Publishers is a division of WMU®,
an international organization that challenges Christian
believers to understand and be radically involved in
God's mission. For more information about WMU,
go to www.wmu.com. More information
about New Hope books may be found at
www.newhopepublishers.com. New Hope books
may be purchased at your local bookstore.